CMO TO CRO

CMO TO CRO

THE REVENUE TAKEOVER BY
THE NEXT GENERATION EXECUTIVE

MIKE GELLER | ROLLY KEENAN | BRANDI STARR

LIONCREST
PUBLISHING

CMO TO CRO

The Revenue Takeover by the Next Generation Executive

ISBN 978-1-5445-1781-0 *Hardcover*

978-1-5445-1780-3 *Paperback*

978-1-5445-1779-7 *Ebook*

When we talked about how to write our dedication, Mike suggested that we use one line: "To our target audience." And in a way, that would be the right amount of humor and truth for us as a management team. However, with an opportunity to really dedicate our efforts in this book to people who deserve it, we'll forgo the humor and truth and deliver some gratitude.

Our work in this book, from the first page through the last, comes from the authors, the Tegrita Management Team, but that work rests on the work done every day by Tegrita consultants. So we're dedicating this book to all the consultants who are or who have been a part of Tegrita. You have worked alongside us, inspired us, and brought us to this point so we could get the word out that it's time for a Revenue Takeover.

We are grateful to you all, and we understand that the message we are delivering to leaders in Marketing and Sales and to entrepreneurs is a result of all your work. Our many clients have presented challenges for us to tackle, and in our pursuits together as a team, we've accomplished great things. In our book, CMO to CRO, we hope we've tied all those accomplishments together.

Thank you.

CONTENTS

INTRODUCTION

The buying landscape has changed in a big way. The technologies have changed. Most of all, customer expectations have changed. We're living in a digital transaction world that rises and falls on the success or failure of the customer experience, *CX*.

Over in the consumer world, some companies are getting CX right. Want to know what to order for dinner or watch on TV? Which car to buy or home mortgage to go with? These decisions are just a few clicks away because those industries figured out that delivery of a consistent, seamless, end-to-end experience is what customers want.

So why are so many companies still selling like it's 1999? They tackle the digital game from every direction, from Marketing to Sales, Customer Support to Customer Success, but most are behind the curve and struggling to catch up.

And without a unified strategy, the end result is inconsistent, disjointed, and frustrating for customers.

The customer isn't the only one who's frustrated. Business leaders, and especially Marketing, want the rewards of getting the customer experience right. If only they could find a way to bring together all the tech, all the people—all the *work*—to optimize the customer experience...now that would be a game changer. It would change how they market, how they sell, and how they make money for the business.

The "solution" seems to be out there. People are talking about it, especially people who think they have it. Martech experts in industry magazines and blogs, at conferences, and on webinars believe they have a quick fix for your customer experience challenges. If you look closely, however, the solutions they offer are usually just more technology. They're Band-Aids that might fix one issue, but don't consider the bigger problem—how companies are organized, or *disorganized*, around the people and technology responsible for customer experience.

MORE TECH IS NOT THE ANSWER

Throwing technology at a problem just leads to more technology to manage. You might have too much technology, not enough, or the wrong technology. And when you think you have the right mix, you realize the people supporting it don't talk to each other. They're playing for different teams with different goals and different leadership. Everybody owns a little piece of CX, but no one owns *all* of it. Like a bunch of specialists treating different symptoms, but no one doctor addressing the patient's disease.

This isn't a big company problem or a small company problem, and it isn't limited to any one industry. It's a problem that's happening all over. A consistent, end-to-end customer experience *is* possible—and when done right, it leads to more customers buying more products.

Because of the transactional nature of their customer interactions, consumer businesses are better positioned to let technology drive the customer experience and put their departments, people, and processes behind it. Still, few get it right, and fewer still B2B companies even come close. We've seen clients manage *parts* of CX very well. However, a holistic, end-to-end solution—which is what we propose in this book—is the surest way to solve your CX problem.

In the simplest terms, we believe the key to effective, sustainable customer experience relies on four actions:

1. Get the right technology.
2. Create a revolutionary revenue operations team.
3. Align leadership compensation and goals.
4. Introduce a new kind of CRO.

This may sound revolutionary—even a little "out there." While it's a big shift from what most companies do now, they (and you) can get there from here.

THE REVENUE PROBLEM

This situation offers a huge opportunity for marketing leadership. If you're a chief marketing officer or a director of marketing, or have a leadership position somewhere along the marketing chain of command, you already know how different teams and technologies impact the customer experience. You also understand the connection between CX, more customers, more sales, and revenue growth.

Customer experience is a key lever to revenue growth. Companies need revenue to pay salaries, fund projects, and invest in infrastructure and research and development. Companies want to turn a profit for their shareholders too. Without revenue, none of that happens. Ultimately, the CEO is responsible for revenue, but unless you're a startup, that's not who's out there closing deals. CEOs look to Sales for revenue, and more recently, to digital technologies and the teams that own them. But still, Sales is #1 in the CEO's "big book of revenue." For decades—generations—Sales has sat proudly on the revenue throne. Businesses have depended on salespeople to bring in the cash; they also blame Sales when revenue goals are missed.

We want to let you in on a secret: Sales no longer sits on that throne. They abdicated the revenue throne a long time ago. Salespeople are only one piece of the revenue puzzle. They know it. Marketing knows it. Somebody needs to say it out loud—and do something about those missed revenue goals. In this book, we'll show you what you can do. It's not fair to the CEO to keep missing revenue goals, it's not fair to Sales to take the blame, and it's not fair to Marketing to have to stand aside. Because marketing leaders are the solution to the customer experience *and*, therefore, the revenue problem.

Customer experience is a key lever to revenue growth.

REVENUE TAKEOVER

In the simplest terms, most revenue comes from sales. Some sales (lowercase "s") are driven by Sales (uppercase "S"), but a massive number of transactions have nothing to do with the capital S salespeople or the sales department. Transactions that generate revenue are largely driven by customer experience. A positive customer experience turns prospects into customers and customers into repeat buyers.

While revenue comes from sales, which are more often than not driven by customer experience, CX is driven by technology. Yet when it comes to anything that's more than just a pair of socks, most companies treat the customer experience as if Sales is still on the revenue throne and all that technology doesn't even exist.

Marketers know this is true. Some are trying to do something about it—like finding the best tech to solve their problems. But if that's all they're doing, it's not enough. Unless marketers want to be left behind, they're looking at major changes in how marketing operates: how it's structured and how the company is structured to support it. That's the big scary news because—we know—leaders have enough on their plates, and a company re-org is the last thing on a CMO's mind. But there's good news too.

The good news is that more marketers have identified the problem. They just haven't found a solution. The truth is, the same challenges *caused* by technology—the proliferation of tech that doesn't always work together to create a consistent customer experience—can also be *solved* by technology. We know this from working with company after company and seeing the impact small steps in the right direction can make. However, few are brave enough to take the giant leap required to make a comprehensive and lasting impact on their CX problem. Instead of scrambling to catch up, marketers have to get behind—*behind the tech*.

It starts with Marketing. Not with Sales and not with IT. The CMO has the depth and breadth of knowledge about marketing, CX, and revenue to put a plan into action that leverages tech holistically and intelligently to help the business make sales, help the CEO meet revenue goals, and confidently seat themselves on the revenue throne. *To effectively go from CMO to CRO.*

This CRO isn't the chief revenue officer in the traditional sense. They don't track revenue. They provide leadership to drive it.

In a Revenue Takeover, the CRO doesn't track revenue. They provide leadership to *drive* it.

NO, THIS IS NOT ANOTHER MAGIC PILL

What we're proposing is not a magic pill. As consultants, we help marketers get to the root of the problem and fix it from the ground up. We've spent the last couple of decades working with businesses to organize, manage, and leverage marketing technology to drive revenue. We've seen what works and what doesn't. We've seen the organizational challenges businesses face, especially as they affect marketing, the customer experience, and ultimately, revenue. A Revenue Takeover is hard work, but the results are worth it. And no one is in a better position to make it happen than a marketing leader.

We've seen firsthand what the elements of a Revenue Takeover can do for businesses and the people who work there.

It doesn't just change the company; it changes people's lives. Formerly frustrated marketing people sleep better at night. Salespeople breathe easier. And CEOs win more and worry less.

We're always looking for ways to give back to the business community and share what we know outside of our consultant roles. Along with helping companies one at a time, we seek out opportunities to help companies as a whole. To honor our own principles and be true to who we are, we're morally obligated to get this information out to as many people as possible. That's what inspired us to write this book.

We wrote this book for marketers—people like you who have had enough and are ready for a fresh approach to an old problem. We are going to show you how to recalibrate, revamp, and restructure how your organization handles revenue-producing functions. In Part 1, "The Problem," we'll lay out the current situation. Don't be surprised if you see yourself in some of the scenarios. These problems affect just about every company we've worked with. Then, in Part 2, "The Future," we'll talk about the possibilities— what your business could look like if you're willing to take the steps we lay out in Part 3, "How You Get There." Part 3 introduces the Revenue Takeover in four phases:

1. Have the right technology in place to optimize the customer experience.

2. Create a revenue operations team to own and manage that technology holistically.

3. Line up your organization's Marketing, Sales, Support, Success, and Revenue Operations goals—collectively, the *CX goals*—behind the technology.

4. Instate a leader with experience on CX teams, working knowledge of CX technology (now Revenue Technology, or RevTech), a clear understanding of how the customer experience drives revenue, and the courage to lead a Revenue Takeover—a new type of CRO.

You might be tempted to skip ahead to Part 3, but we think you'll miss out on a lot. To do what's necessary, you really need to understand the commonality so many companies share around CX and how much better it can be for people with the courage to execute a Revenue Takeover. You will have to put your heart into it. You can't just go through the motions.

So let's jump into Part 1, Chapter 1, "Enough Is Enough." Because that's how a lot of executives, salespeople, and especially marketers are feeling right now.

We're always looking for ways to give back to the business community and share what we know outside of our consultant roles. Along with helping companies one at a time, we seek out opportunities to help companies as a whole. To honor our own principles and be true to who we are, we're morally obligated to get this information out to as many people as possible.

PART I

THE PROBLEM

The current situation at many companies is a sense of frustration over the lack of cohesiveness between customer experience strategies, CX department goals that don't work together to align with business goals, a lot of customer experience technology without a holistic strategy, and a lack of visibility, communication, and collaboration between CX teams. Let's talk about these problems and why they matter.

CHAPTER 1

ENOUGH IS ENOUGH

The definition of insanity is doing the same thing over and over again and expecting a different result.

—UNKNOWN

Sound familiar? This is what a lot of marketers do every day—operate in a continuous state of insanity. If this is you, it's no wonder you're frustrated. You feel like you're spinning your wheels but getting mediocre results, with never enough time to come up for air.

Marketing is under pressure to help other departments grow. Grow awareness. Grow engagement. Grow the customer base. Land and expand with more products and services at every customer site. Grow *revenue*.

These growth goals don't always go as planned. Sometimes

they aren't realistic to begin with. More often, they're poorly imagined and executed. Plans for growth, no matter which department they come from, have one thing in common: they all rely on Marketing to help achieve them. When they fail, everyone's looking at Marketing. But when departments fail to meet their goals, it's seldom Marketing's fault. They usually don't have any input on those goals or a say in whether they have the resources to meet them. Think about it: *how often are you consulted about other departments' goals before they're assigned to you?*

> When departments fail to meet their goals, it's seldom Marketing's fault (though they often get the blame). Think about it: *how often are you consulted about other departments' goals before they're assigned to you?*

Marketing is feeling a lot of pain, and so are other departments tasked with the customer experience. But alone in their silos, they aren't aware of each other's pain. And while some departments can muddle through the pain and still attain a level of success, Marketing is stuck with unattainable goals because many jobs it's tasked with rely on other departments and the information and resources those other departments own.

The function so many other departments rely on for growth—*Marketing*—is uniquely positioned to be the catalyst for change yet is often overlooked to lead the change.

OPERATING IN SILOS

Marketing has a lot of contact with prospects and customers at many levels, and they leverage that contact to support the needs of other departments. Yet, they have little control over it or over the conversations everyone else has with the customer. Marketing owns some of the technology, but groups like Sales, Customer Support, and Customer Success own some too, and some is owned by IT.

Each department operates in its own silo with little regard for how what they do affects other departments. Meanwhile, Marketing's racing around, generating interest, churning out leads, and doing whatever else is required to help other departments succeed. Marketing sees how their goals clash with other departments' goals. They also see how other departments' goals conflict with another's, and another's, and another's...and how they sometimes clash with the goals of the company. They see how their demands compete for Marketing's resources. It's exhausting because marketers are caught up in a losing game.

Many industry leaders and analysts talk about centering their businesses around customer experience; having an executive and a team focused solely on CX is the "shiny new thing." But while everyone talks about customer experience, no one talks about the *whole* experience. Even CX teams fall short because they tend to focus on *components* of the experience and not the whole experience. They may be focused on creating an amazing web experience, for example, and there's a disconnect between that and other customer touches. They might create an interactive, highly personalized experience on the website, but it doesn't trickle down to Marketing. Since Marketing doesn't have access to the same tools, it has none of the data. The amazing web experience starts off well, but when it comes to nurturing the traffic, nothing's happening because Marketing isn't connected. If visitors to the site become customers, there is no consistent conversation to keep them engaged or support them.

Most companies are doing really well with customer experience in one area or another. If they have a CX team, the most successful part of the customer experience is usually whatever that team is working on. But the success of that one component doesn't carry over to all the others.

THE EXPERIENCE ECONOMY

In this new "experience economy," people assign value to their experience with a brand. The experience isn't with a single element of the brand; it relies on the *whole experience*. If a customer has a bad Marketing experience, a bad Sales experience, or a bad Support experience, they have a negative feeling toward the entire brand. Tacking on added value for the customer is not the solution. That doesn't get to the root of the problem, and to the customer, it presents a disjointed front that doesn't feel right. Additional benefits to the customer aren't experienced the way businesses think they are. The results can be confusing or, worse, repellent.

Think about the last time you had a problem with your phone, or your internet, or your health insurance. You dialed the 800 number, interacted with the voice system, waited on hold for a few minutes, then talked to someone. You explained the problem, and the person said they couldn't help you, but someone else could. *Would you mind being put on hold for a moment while I transfer you?* If you were lucky, the hold time was short, and there was a warm handoff, where the first person introduced you to the next level of support and gave them your name and a brief description of the problem. More likely, the transfer was cold: you were put into a different phone queue, and the person you ended up speaking with didn't know who you were or why you were calling. After several transfers, you finally got to the right person, and each time you had to give them the exact same information. Maybe at some point during these transfers, you ended up with the first person you talked to. You explained the problem again, and they realized they could have handled your problem without transferring you at all. Maybe they took care of it. But sometimes you get to the right person, they put you on hold (*just for a moment*), annnnnnd...you're disconnected.

Each person you talked to probably thought they were doing

a great job. Every one of them was very thorough yet expedient in collecting your information and transferring you to the next queue, so from their point of view, they appear to be doing everything right. That's not how you saw it, though, because by the end of the experience, you've provided your name, phone number, email address, and your problem to a dozen different people, and frankly, you don't ever want to deal with that company again.

This is your experience within *just one department*—Support. Imagine calling that same company to speak with Sales about getting a new product or service. Or to speak with Billing because there's a mistake on your last bill. Now those departments might provide you with terrific experiences, but because you just spent an hour with Support, you are not impressed. In your mind, the whole brand has been tarnished, and you're thinking about switching to a different internet provider, or phone provider, or insurance company.

TECHNOLOGY "FIXES" AREN'T THE ANSWER

Symptoms are signs of a bigger problem. When you hear that website engagement is low, that's a symptom. Low conversion is a symptom. Make a list of your "problems." How many are actually symptoms? Treating the symptoms doesn't cure the problem; it *masks* the problem. And now, the problem will manifest itself somewhere else. It's like swatting flies with a baseball bat, thinking you're solving your fly problem. Guess what? The flies are still there, hidden under the rubble you created swinging that bat. Still, businesses keep reaching for the baseball bat, usually in the form of new technology. But the technology that drives better web behavior or improves conversion rates doesn't *cure* anything, and it doesn't solve the fly problem.

Yet, companies continue to invest in new tech. They install a new marketing automation platform, expecting to increase velocity and conversion and drive new leads, and they're puzzled when it doesn't solve all the nurture issues. Frustrated, they install something else, but that doesn't solve the problem either. Without a plan for how all this technology works together and aligns with business goals, it's like buying new baseball bats when what's really needed is a bomb squad. In the meantime, more tech creates more work. People have to figure out how to use every new tool and make it work with all the other tools. And they hope and pray that the new technology delivers results fast—before someone calls it ineffective or a failure and takes it away.

Chances are the right people aren't involved in the decisions, and the right tech isn't being implemented because the real problem hasn't even been identified.

By the way, *you* didn't choose all this technology. People like you who are experiencing the pain—low website engagement, low conversion rates—are seldom consulted about technology buys. You'd love to have some input on what might work best to solve the problem or at least treat the symptoms, but you aren't even part of that conversation. Someone else makes that decision, and you have to make it work.

WHEN TECHNOLOGY IS EVERYONE'S JOB

A data company we know recently implemented new event technology. The event manager should be overseeing the success of events, analyzing their profitability, and strategizing for future events, but instead she's managing all the coordination between departments and handling the logistics of the event programs.

There were gaps in the implementation, and the manager had to figure out which existing technologies and processes were affected and how they had to be updated. She drove the conversation with the IT team to integrate the new tech with their marketing automation platform so she could automate emails, among other things. This is not what an event manager signs up for, yet they are often tasked with these responsibilities. She wanted time to focus on using the system to deliver on the business objectives, but with no one in place who understood event management's needs enough to handle the technical piece, she was obligated to take on the job.

The most negative impact of this situation was the huge demand on the manager's time. This cut into her availability to launch events, so she had to put in a lot more time to meet the department's goals. And while she was working through the integration, processes that should have been automated had to be done manually. She and her team put in long hours during the fine-tuning of the implementation and integration, doing a job that shouldn't have been dumped on them in the first place.

So much new technology—along with the disconnect between departments, their goals, and the technology—is hard on people. It affects morale. Employees don't feel valued, and they don't feel like they're contributing to the company's goals. *They're* disconnected. Marketers are in a battle with other departments to get what they need to meet their goals. That doesn't leave any time for strategic thinking. There is no personal or professional growth—it's like being a hamster on a wheel going around and around and getting nowhere.

Marketing leaders often spend time working *in* the business instead of *on* the business. They don't have enough time for strategy. They are tasked with driving growth, yet a small fraction (if any) of their time is spent doing that. Functional managers within the marketing team try to keep up with what's in front of them. Their days are spent on whatever's pressing, timely, and requires their attention *right now.* The volume of immediate tasks is so overwhelming that any kind of analysis that could be pushed up to assist with future intelligence and strategy is a luxury no one can afford. These middle managers work on whatever has the greatest visibility across the organization. *What are people expecting, and how do we do it well enough to meet their minimum expectations with the time and resources available?* Mediocrity becomes the accepted norm because everybody's just trying to keep their heads above water. As long as they're going in the direction that makes most of the people happy, even if they're only taking baby steps, that's good enough.

Highly qualified, mid-career marketers are doing work they shouldn't be, plus they're supposed to do more with the same or fewer resources. People want to feel like they're part of something bigger, something with meaning. You can't expect them to devote forty or more hours of their lives every week to work that's beneath their abilities or that doesn't seem to matter. Eventually, people in this situation leave. Some marketing departments see an 80 percent turnover year after year. People who leave aren't always going to more progressive companies. Sometimes they've mastered a skill that they see going away in the business to be replaced by some new tech, so they go to another company that needs a person with that skill. Sometimes they seek out opportunities at businesses with less tech so they can do things the way they've been doing them for years. They want to be productive, and they want less stress. When people leave, they take their knowledge with them. All the training you've invested in them, and the time you've paid them to learn on the job, and all the organizational knowledge they've accumulated goes right out the door. You can replace them with an expert, and that new person is still not going to be up to speed on your business.

JACKS (AND JILLS) OF ALL
TRADES, MASTERS OF NONE

A VP of Marketing's annual goals were all around driving revenue from email marketing. This was supposed to be the solution that reduced their marketing budgets and made their store owners more effective. They bought a marketing automation platform and slated only one person to manage it, who was also the copywriter and not the most technical person. This was the VP's only report who had any alignment to email marketing, so the success of the program—and the department's annual goals—rose or fell on her abilities. Because the VP had a technical background, she ended up taking on the role of administrator, running most of the campaigns and building and troubleshooting emails. She did nothing a VP of Marketing would normally do. Eventually, she went to work for the competitor where she could take on the role of VP, do the work she wanted to do, and because of her technical background, command a high salary.

YOU'RE NOT CRAZY

You got stuck in an insane business model that hasn't caught on to the fact that the 20th century ended decades ago. It's time to move on. It's time to say, "Enough is enough." It's time to take charge and make the big changes that bring CX and revenue growth into the 21st century. Marketing leaders are uniquely positioned to make the first move, and with this book, you have the guidance.

The major issues that have brought us to this point and why they matter are the subject of the next four chapters. One is relying on technology to solve symptoms instead of building a strategy to attack underlying problems. Another is a lack of visibility and collaboration between departments to optimize the customer experience. Before we get to those, let's look at why companies tend to measure the wrong things and how that feeds into other issues.

HIGH PAY, LOW VALUE

Two directors at a business we worked with spent their days writing copy and editing emails on topics they clearly were not familiar with instead of doing what a person at that level should be doing. The people on their teams hadn't been out of college long and weren't trained to take on the tasks that the directors need them to do. These high-level, highly paid employees with decades of experience were essentially spending their time doing the same thing their inexperienced new hires were doing. One of the directors left, but the other one is still there, churning away.

CHAPTER 2

WHAT GETS MEASURED GETS DONE

There is nothing so useless as doing efficiently that which should not be done at all.

—PETER DRUCKER

At a company we consulted for, a marketing manager's success was measured by the number of Marketing Qualified Leads (MQLs) generated by her team. There was a quarterly bonus for the manager if her team met the goal. Three years in a row, they exceeded it. Every marketing manager in the company met their lead goals too, though some did so by *relaxing* their definitions of what constituted Marketing Qualified; they did not want to jeopardize their quarterly bonuses.

Overall, the conversion rate from Marketing Qualified to Sales Accepted Leads was low, and the rate decreased further as the leads moved through the sales cycle. Revenue generated at the end of the cycle did not justify the marketing budget for generating qualified leads. In the fourth year, the CMO decided that marketing should no longer be measured on leads generated but on the percentage of conversions from Marketing Qualified Leads to Sales Accepted Leads. The percentage was arbitrary and much higher than any of the previous quarters' percentages.

The marketing manager's and her counterparts' bonuses were then tied to the new metric. Now, Sales Accepted is actually a better metric for sales success and revenue than the number of qualified leads, and the manager knew this. She was excited to contribute even more visibly to the company's success, but she'd have to change the way her team qualified leads. She put more stringent guidelines in place to ensure that every lead her team sent to Sales had been fully vetted—in her mind, every lead should have been readily accepted by a salesperson.

The salespeople, however, were reluctant to accept all the new leads. Sales didn't know the criteria each marketing manager was using to vet the leads, and they had received so many bad leads over the years that they were skeptical that anything had changed. They also knew that since these leads had been deemed Sales Accepted, they would be expected to close a higher percentage of them. Sales had no process for what they did with any of the leads they accepted, either. There was no service-level agreement around how to manage them, so even a Sales Accepted Lead that actually *was* accepted by a salesperson wasn't automatically pursued.

The marketing manager was extremely frustrated. She believed that Sales didn't always value the leads her team provided and that salespeople rejected many that they should have accepted. She had no way to track her team's progress toward the metric and no way to know if she was going to reach her objective. Because of the lack of infrastructure and misalignment of goals, neither the historically overachieving marketing manager nor any of her colleagues received a bonus.

In the end, the marketing managers were unhappy, and their low morale was felt throughout the marketing teams. No one knew whether they had done a good job. The company also missed out on new customer acquisitions and sales: because the salespeople were reluctant to accept the qualified leads that Marketing had pushed nearly to the finish line, prospects went elsewhere. Some leads weren't pursued at all, and even meetings that had been scheduled for salespeople were missed. Because Marketing and Sales were measured on different criteria that did not align, opportunities for revenue and company growth were missed.

Their intentions to increase revenue were understandable, but their efforts failed. The worst outcome of the fiasco was the effect on the customer experience. Both Sales and Marketing worried more about their quotas and blamed each other when it didn't happen—the customer experience wasn't even part of the picture. The process was not holistically viewed, planned, executed, or measured with the point of view of the customer in mind.

MISALIGNED METRICS

Every department has measures. In some cases, those measures are seemingly aligned. In the marketing manager example, Marketing's goal was to generate leads that would be accepted by Sales. The percentage of leads actually accepted was the measure. Sales' goal was to work the leads and turn them into sales. The percentage of sales made was the measure. On the surface, these goals seemed to be aligned. However, there was a kind of invisible wall between the departments and their goals that no one had taken into account.

The goals of the organization and every department are not always aligned. Even when they are, the processes for achieving individual goals may be counterproductive. What gets measured gets done. But unless everything you're measuring is aligned, you may be measuring and doing the wrong things.

> What gets measured gets done. But unless everything you're measuring is aligned, you may be measuring and doing the wrong things.

GOALS ARE DECIDED INDIVIDUALLY AND HANDED DOWN

Typically, the C-suite hands down goals and objectives, and everyone has to figure out where they fit. But each role in the C-suite has its own individual charge. The Head of Marketing focuses on driving qualified lead generation. The Head of Sales focuses on closing deals. The Head of IT focuses on corporate initiatives that support the business company-wide. The siloed mentality starts at the top and sets the stage for departmental silos. Every year these senior executives get into a room and come up with business objectives for each department. Sometimes these objectives are arbitrary. They're often in conflict. Goals are handed to their departments. Managers, directors, and team leaders are then directed to allocate their time and resources toward hitting them (the goals, not the executives). They may be incentivized on their success.

The problem is exacerbated when an organization brings in a heavy hitter to head up a department. The CEO is impressed with a hotshot's performance at another company and hires them to repeat that success. So, this new person signs up for a few years, and they have a package—

usually a sum of money, but there can be other rewards, like stock—tied to making the department a success. If they want to reap all the rewards, they have to meet the goals laid out in the contract. They're super-focused on satisfying the contract and less concerned with how their actions affect other departments' success. They may not run roughshod over them, but their main goal is not going to be communication, corporate strategy, or alignment. These individual actors do their thing, collect their packages, and move on to another company. In the meantime, they stepped all over any momentum you had with enhancing the customer experience and meeting your department's goals.

An extreme version of this happens when venture capitalists start a business or get involved with an existing one. They have a goal of taking a company from, say, nothing to $50 million. They put in leadership that's successful in their specialties. The fact is, individual success in every department doesn't always lead to revenue success or growth success for the whole company.

DYSFUNCTION IN THE C-SUITE

Every company has a method for determining executive goals. The dysfunction you see at the department level is just as common at the C-suite level—regardless of company size or industry. Companies bring in rock stars to fix their problems with little to no consideration for other leaders and their objectives. The new Head of Sales is brought in for three years and promised a big package if she can hit the goal—*and don't worry about who you have to step on to make it happen.* Ignore the CMO? *Sure.* Priority access to IT resources? *Why not.* Okay if you throw the rest of the company into turmoil? *Who cares? Get it done, collect your package, and move on. We'll worry about the fallout later.*

This happens more often than you might think. We were in a meeting with a CMO last year. We'd been working with some of her people in the different marketing departments—Marcom, CX, marketing operations, lead gen—to understand how they did their jobs. Now it was time to talk strategy. We stepped through our findings and then launched into all the key opportunities for improvement we had identified. She was vibing with everything we said.

Toward the end of the meeting, she got up and closed the door. "Listen," she said, "I'm going to be transparent with you. Everything you've just said is amazing, but most of it isn't new to me. I *know* we have these problems." She sat down, thought for a moment, and continued: "The biggest issue, though, is the one you can't see. *Nothing I say holds water.* I've been here three years, but last year the company brought in a new Chief Revenue Officer. He was highly recruited and cost us a lot. The CEO basically gave him carte blanche authority to do whatever he felt necessary to turn the department around."

The CMO knew the industry and knew the business. She was aware of the issues and was working toward fixing them, but suddenly she was on the outside. The CRO instituted changes that made him look good but didn't make sense for the company. His first objective was around a product that wasn't selling. To fix it, he needed a better way to measure the velocity of leads and opportunities in the sales funnel. The company had been using a CRM system for this. The system, which had been in use for many years, was integrated with many other systems across the company and functioned well for everyone else. The CRO brought in a different CRM that didn't talk to those other systems. It worked well for that *one* problem, and product sales exceeded everyone's expectations. Sales made their numbers, and the CRO looked like a hero.

While they were celebrating, the rest of the company was in a tailspin. Marketing's lead platform was integrated with the old CRM, so leads weren't going to the salespeople. Sure, they were closing deals they already had in their buckets, but Marketing was spinning its wheels, generating leads that no one followed up on. Finance didn't have any visibility into the opportunities that closed. Every department that touched Sales was impacted. The CMO was powerless to do anything to help her marketing people. No matter what they did, they would never get credit. To the rest of the company, she and her entire department looked like failures.

This wasn't the first time we'd heard this story. It happens at companies everywhere. At another business, a similar situation resulted in 75 percent of a department leaving the company. Their efforts, they realized, were irrelevant. When people feel like their work doesn't matter, they move on. Sometimes people stay and sabotage the company. When these C-suite decisions are made, the outcome is never good for most employees.

DYSFUNCTION ON THE FLOOR

In big companies, objectives roll downhill. They start with the package promised to the executive over a particular function or department, and everyone is expected to fall in line. One example of this is a major motorcycle corporation that brought in a new Head of Manufacturing and tasked him with the goal of shrinking the overall product cost. His compensation was tied directly to making that happen.

Meanwhile, other departments were rolling out a new option to customers. They were allowing them to design the product exactly to their preferences—basically building the bike of their dreams. This objective had been handed down before the new guy ever showed up. Marketing had been hard at work advertising this option, and it was starting to gain traction. Their metrics were looking good.

Unfortunately, their metrics did not align with the goals

of the Head of Manufacturing. Allowing customers to choose their options may have been a fantastic long-term strategy for the company, but in the short-term, the most noticeable effect was an increase in manufacturing costs. The whole campaign was trashed, a plant closed, and other departments' goals weren't met. The Head of Manufacturing achieved his objective, though. He even got a bonus.

Often, individual departments aren't only unaware of how *their* objectives interfere with those of other departments—they basically aren't even *aware* of those other goals and seldom think about other departments at all. And each department has tunnel vision when it comes to what they believe is most important. They focus on their goals and how they're measured and often compensated.

In the case of the iconic motorcycle manufacturer, the new head was focused on one objective. His department was aligned to one goal, and their metrics were tied to that goal. They were compensated on those metrics. All the while, Marketing was probably focused on generating some excitement around the product and building fan engagement. They had brand loyalists who would jump on the chance to order a custom bike tailored to their preferences, so it made sense for Marketing to put money and effort around that initiative. Heads of departments don't intentionally choose objectives that undermine other departments—they just don't consider them. Instead, they interpret how their department impacts the business goals.

In another example, an automotive components manufacturer had a goal to launch fifteen new products in 2019. By the fourth quarter, they had only launched seven, so they scrambled to launch eight more products by the end of the year. Marketing, in turn, suddenly had to come up with product launch campaigns for each new product in record time. Instead of their usual high standards, they had to crank through these campaigns to meet their metrics. You can imagine how successful those product launches were and how proud the marketers were (not) to hit their goals. But they hit them, and they got their bonuses. The product people hit their numbers too. But no one felt good about any of it. It all looked good on paper, but for the company and the people who worked there, it could hardly be called a success.

THE PROBLEM WITH ANNUAL GOALS

Maybe this story sounds familiar. There is a company where, every year, each employee has an annual performance review. They sit down with their manager to review all the goals they had set the previous year and talk about the progress they had made. Maybe they get a bonus and a raise. Sometimes they get a promotion. Other times, the person is let go. It all depends on that annual review.

Then they move on to the next year's goals. Each department has maybe five business goals, and the employee has to come up with five objectives to work on to support each business goal. So if one of the goals is to "build brand awareness," the person outlines the specific actions they will take over the next year to contribute to that goal. Likewise, people in product development and customer service choose their individual objectives to impact their departmental goals. The problem is that all these objectives are individually selected and, for the most part, universally accepted by the manager. There is no team discussion, no holistic view, and ultimately no synergy between each person's objectives and how they contribute to the goal. And that's *within the department*. Of course, the same is true between departments: no discussion, no holistic view, and no synergy between their goals either. This leads to duplication of effort, contradictory goals, and gaps in activity focused on the company's business objectives and revenue goals.

Each department head focuses on what *they* believe is important to achieve the overall organizational goals. There is no collaboration with other departments directly impacted by the work they're doing and no understanding of the effects they have on other departments' goals. It's not that department heads are egomaniacs—they are compensated for hitting specific metrics that aren't aligned with other departments. Even if a leader's goals don't make sense for other departments, it's counterproductive for that person to look at *the* big picture instead of looking at *their* big picture. Compensation is a major factor in how individuals focus their attention, and it usually trumps what actually makes sense.

You would think someone has their eye on the best interests of the company as a whole, right? The CEO, maybe? Nope, because she may be a hired gun too. That's right—the person in charge often has their own agenda, like hitting goals that set them up for their next career move. Typically, they're looking for a gigantic exit. If you confront the CEO, they will tell you, "Don't hate the player, hate the game."

BUSINESS IS DIGITIZED, BUT *THE* BUSINESS IS ANALOG

Over the last ten or more years, businesses have had multiyear projects to go through digital transformations. What that actually means varies from place to place, but the idea is using new technology that's probably in the cloud to provide a better customer experience. A lot of times, these projects involve legacy systems that organizations built themselves, whose upkeep and maintenance doesn't make sense because there are so many fantastic off-the-shelf products available. These products have literally transformed how customers interact with businesses. Beneath the surface problem of piling new tech on old systems lies a more serious issue within the business structure itself.

Behind the scenes, departments have remained the same. The business units in place today—not the people, but the *structures*—were essentially designed for an analog world. Businesses have gone through various digital transformations, but they're operating in an environment that predates the internet.

Business is digitized, yet departments are still working in an analog way with disparate goals because of how they're structured and how goals are handed down. Despite the technology evolution, neither department structure nor goals have changed. The parallel is that because of the digital environment and the way that technology has impacted things, businesses can't organize themselves or set goals the same way they used to. Within this outdated structure, there is a massive opportunity for evolution.

With software robots and AI, information is connected on the back end. It's digitized and connected for an optimal customer experience. The technology in use today allows businesses to do more work with the same number of people. We are nearing a future where marketing segmentation could be generated by AI based on the data that you collect. From a sales standpoint, there is software that will automatically record everything in the CRM relating to whomever you're talking to about an opportunity.

FRONT OFFICE TODAY

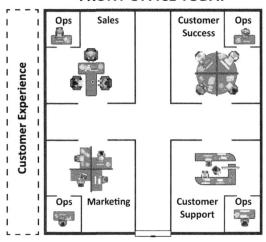

FRONT OFFICE TOMORROW

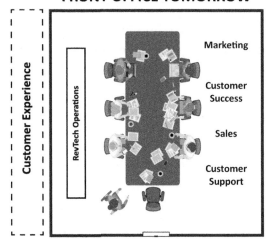

Today's typical front office reflects an analog world, with each department sitting at their own individual table, setting their own goals, and communicating the work they've accomplished to other departments "after the fact." Contrast that model with the front office of tomorrow, which reflects a modern, digital world where everyone is sitting at the same table, aligning their goals in real time before the work begins.

Customers used to interact with businesses in an analog way, so companies set themselves up internally that way. Through every moment of information and interaction, selling, service, or support, the digitization began slowly, and then suddenly there was a huge move toward customers interacting solely through technology. Businesses did not restructure themselves to match that shift.

ORGANIZED BY FUNCTION

Though many departments affect the customer experience, they are all part of the traditional organizational structure, set up by function. Each department's scope is narrow. Even the customer experience department focuses mainly on customer interactions through the purchase process. That includes online shopping, filling out a form at an event, going to a physical store, or speaking with a salesperson. No one focuses on the entire experience a customer has with the business. At some companies, the CX department has the authority to get involved with other departments and how they interact with customers, but there is no company-wide strategy.

Each department has its own budget too. The largest portion of Marketing's budget is poured into demand generation efforts: content syndication, digital advertising, event sponsorships; money gets spent based on objectives. The organizational structure within marketing teams is very much aligned to the different organizational priorities. Multiple marketing managers might be focused on demand generation, while others are focused on cross-selling and upselling or win-backs and renewals. Well-rounded staffing has three types of managers focused on the three goals of marketing: retaining current customers, generating more revenue from them, and generating new customers.

But most marketing departments are not organized this way. They might have a single marketing manager who covers everything with undefined goals. They might have a large demand gen team and one person who does everything else.

HIGHER EXPECTATIONS, FEWER RESOURCES

Marketing team size is decreasing. Marketing budgets have fluctuated, going up, down, and flattening from year to year. Often, Marketing is expected to do more, show higher returns, and generate more revenue with the same budget and fewer people. Technology is supposed to make this possible. The challenge is that companies don't account for having people to run the tech. They don't plan for proper training and ramp-up so people really understand the technology. They're not even clear about the goals of the technology they implement. If you don't think about the people behind the tech for the tech to be effective, your plan is destined to fail. For example, if you buy a marketing automation platform, you buy the technology. Most companies have an implementation plan but no plan for ensuring employees understand all of the new system's capabilities. There is no strategy within the time and money budget for including resources to learn, manage, and run it.

Forty-six percent of respondents expect their Martech budget and investment to increase slightly, and 18 percent expect it to increase greatly.[1]

Technology doesn't run itself. Someone has to do something with it. A rough estimate for new tech planning is that you will spend four times the cost of the technology on training and management. If you spend $20,000 on the tech, budget $80,000 for training, external consulting—everything you need to get the full value of the technology. To get your return on investment, you have to invest in all the right things. You might even have to dedicate someone full-time to realize the technology's—and your investment's—potential.

Leveraging the technology for other uses in addition to the main reason you purchased it may also require a different skillset. If you have people on the team who have been doing the same job manually for years and have lim-

---

1   Walker Sands, "State of Marketing Technology 2019: Exploring the Trends that Make Martech Tick," 2019, https://1bnznaaikg11oqsn3tvx88r9-wpengine.netdna-ssl.com/wp-content/uploads/2019/09/WalkerSands_2019StateofMerch_DataReport_WSRB.pdf.

ited technical aptitude, you can't just hand them some advanced technology and expect miracles. When you're solving a tech gap, you have to solve the skill gap. You may have people with very strategic minds but no technical aptitude put into these roles. You can train them, hire new people, or outsource the work.

Some organizations try to manage on their own, and they struggle. Other organizations understand their limitations and bring in external support. A third type of organization understands its limitations, does what it can in-house, and hires a third party to close the gaps. Most companies, unfortunately for them, do not recognize their limitations, and they fail to train the people they have or bring in others to fill the gaps or manage the tech for them.

MISALIGNED, MISMEASURED, AND MISSED OPPORTUNITIES

Technology is supposed to allow Marketing to do more with less. But when everything behind the tech is misaligned with the company's goals and mismeasured as to its true effectiveness, you miss out on the opportunity to reach your goals. What gets measured gets done, so you better be measuring the right things. Otherwise, your work will be a waste of time or, worse, counterproductive.

There's a way to fix this problem, and we're going to take

you through it step by step. For now, let's look at how technology affects the customer experience.

CHAPTER 3

TOO MUCH TECH, NOT ENOUGH STRATEGY

I suppose it is tempting, if the only tool you have is a hammer, to treat everything as if it were a nail.

—ABRAHAM MASLOW

You need an email marketing platform. What do you do? You go out and buy the best in class marketing automation platform. At the same time, the social team is buying the most popular social tool. Meanwhile, digital marketing just acquired a tool for digital placement with functionality that overlaps your new tech *and* social's new tech. Did you really need to buy all this tech? How is it going to work together? And who's going to maintain it?

This is what companies do: whenever there's a problem,

they first try to solve it with what they have, and when that doesn't work, they buy something new *for that problem*. Without fully exploring all the functionality of their current tech or considering what other departments own or are in the process of acquiring.

Everyone sees technology as the quick fix, but nobody has a plan for how that technology completes the *whole*. Where it fits in the Martech stack and how it affects other people, processes, and plans within the organization are rarely even considered. Often, there's a total disconnect. Tools are acquired and installed with no knowledge of other departments' tech or how that technology interacts with your customers.

The problem is multiplied by the number of departments that interact with customers. So it's not just a problem for Marketing—the proliferation of disconnected, overlapping, disjointed technology exists across every department where the natural silos have everyone buying technology to fill their need without even thinking about others' needs or the needs of the greater whole: the business.

BUY FIRST, THINK LATER

This approach to technology acquisition has led to the creation of Martech "monsters." In the spirit of Einstein's notion that "Everything should be made as simple as possible, but not simpler," marketers mistakenly try to solve a single problem with a single tool. The problem is they try to simplify it *too* much. They don't talk to IT, or engineering, or a technologist who might be able to shed some light on why their simple tool may not be such a great idea. So now they've got twenty to thirty tools working together or, in most cases, *not* working together. Like Frankenstein's monster, they're single solutions cobbled together into a scary mess. A *Frankenstack*.

According to Scott Brinker, Founder of ChiefMartec, the average enterprise has a Martech stack consisting of a staggering 91 tools.[2]

When there's a problem, there's an impulse to buy more tech to solve it. That buying instinct overrides the more thoughtful response of researching the problem to discover the source and solve for *it* instead of solving for the symptom. There's no strategy, no holistic approach, and no chance of considering how your tech purchase will affect other tools, other departments, or your company's overall business objectives. And now someone's got to maintain this monster. The technological burden on teams is enormous, and it's not shrinking. It's exploding.

When the first Martech supergraphic was released back in 2011,

2   Kaya Ismail, "Martech Bloat? How Much is Too Much?" *CMS Wire*, August 17, 2018, https://www.cmswire.com/digital-marketing/martech-bloat-how-much-is-too-much/.

ChiefMartec counted 150 platforms. In 2020 the market had grown to accommodate over 8,000 marketing technology solutions.[3]

AVAILABLE TECH IS GROWING, AND SO ARE THE CATEGORIES

Because of the mass proliferation of the tech itself and the categories, marketers find it increasingly difficult to determine the best option to address their specific symptoms and solve their problem. Where you once had three options, you now have thirty-five. Among the thirty-five, you have a hundred variants. They all seem to do the same thing. You evaluate the technology based on the feature set and correlate it against the problem you're trying to solve. That's an easy mistake to make.

Think about the last time you bought a new platform for your website. You looked at all the checklists comparing features and functions on the vendor site and on a G2 crowd vendor comparison site. *Does the system do X?* Yes. That's not good enough because X means something slightly different for each platform. It means something different for how it's implemented and used in your business. If you could assess how the work will actually flow through the

---

3   Scott Brinker, "Marketing Technology Landscape Supergraphic (2020): Martech 5000 — really 8,000, but who's counting?" *The Martech Show*, April 22, 2020, https://chiefmartec.com/2020/04/marketing-technology-landscape-2020-martech-5000.

technology, see if it solves the problem, see if the symptoms disappear, and evaluate the output, you would be able to make a more informed decision.

Working through the procurement process to validate that the technology is going to fix your problem is difficult. It will get harder as more niche tech hits the market and vendors bank on you to fall into that feature trap.

Marketers are spending on tech, too. According to an April [2018] report by Forrester Research, US marketers will increase their investment in marketing technology by 27.1% over the next four years, spending more than $122 billion on marketing tech by 2022.[4]

TECH FOMO

Every year Forbes comes up with a list of all the cool new technology out there that companies are using. The expectation is that everyone should expect to spend more money every year on tech because that's been the trend. Why wouldn't you constantly be shopping around?

Maybe this new tech has AI. Well, if you don't have AI, why don't you? Shouldn't you have it? Everyone else does—or so it seems. Do you really want to be the only kid on the

---

4   Ross Benes, "How Much Are Companies Spending on Technology?" eMarketer.com, August 13, 2018, https://www.emarketer.com/content/how-much-are-companies-spending-on-technology.

block whose technology does not use AI? Wouldn't that be embarrassing? Especially if you don't hit your numbers. If only you had AI...maybe *that* could have saved you.

That's ridiculous. And we're not picking on AI here—pick any new technology. You don't need it unless you actually need it. And even then, you may not need it because you may already own it or something even better.

You can't compare your needs to what other companies are using. You can't look at all the other businesses a vendor serves and think, "If it's good enough for the biggest and best companies in the world, it's good enough for me." That's the kind of mob mentality that leads to terrible buying decisions. What you need depends on the needs of your organization, and a best practice for one company could be a worst practice for yours. Just because your favorite Fortune 500 company is using a technology doesn't mean you should be using it.

Why do marketers buy into this mentality? Probably because they're constantly inundated with the latest and greatest tech by other marketers, salespeople, and industry analysts at conferences they attend and in articles they read. Every year new buzzwords appear. Sometimes they're acronyms. Other times the buzzwords have clues to the problem they claim to solve. They're always just cryptic enough and just tantalizing enough to get your attention and keep you up at night. *Do I have this? Should I have it? What if I don't have it? I better get it right now!*

Vendors can add to the FOMO (fear of missing out) too. They're aware of all the buzzwords, and fearing they might lose customers if they don't offer a product or at least a new feature within their existing product, they'll push their engineers and development people to slap something on to "check the box." Many examples of this exist around AI, and few have been successful. They are often a minimum viable product with a feature set that meets the minimum definition of the buzzword. Yet, vendors push them and marketers without a strategy buy them. Often, they are never even implemented. A side effect of this phenomenon is that resources that should be focused on bug fixes and real product improvements that customers actually need are diverted to haphazard features and solutions to satisfy someone's FOMO.

Buzzwords abound in the marketing world, but it doesn't mean they're all worth investing in. [For example,] 40% of respondents believe AI will continue to be a buzzword in 2019, though only 32% currently use AI or have plans to invest in it this year.[5]

5   Walker Sands, "State of Marketing Technology 2019: Exploring the Trends that Make Martech Tick," 2019, https://1bnznaaikg11oqsn3tvx88r9-wpengine.netdna-ssl.com/wp-content/uploads/2019/09/WalkerSands_2019StateofMerch_DataReport_WSRB.pdf.

FOMO GONE WILD

The head of marketing at a sports organization that Rolly worked with attended a league conference. During a meeting, another team's head of marketing was going on and on about his department's amazing Martech stack. The first head of marketing took notes, and when he got back to the office, he handed the list to his marketing manager with instructions to purchase and implement all of it. The marketing manager brought us in to implement the new tech. One of our first questions was, "Can you tell us why you purchased this particular technology? What goals drove the business decision to switch to this platform, and what outcome do you expect to accomplish?" Their answer was simply, "The CMO went to a conference and found out this is what all the best in class teams are using. He said we have to use it too, but we don't know what we're supposed to accomplish with it." One technology of the stack alone cost $60,000. No one knew what they were supposed to do with it or how they were supposed to get a return on their investment with it.

VENDOR REDIRECT

When you have a problem, no matter what it is, some vendors will try to redirect you to their solution. They want you to use them for everything. Vendors (especially those in the SaaS model) want the technology to be as sticky as possible, so feature usage is especially important. From a vendor standpoint, the more you're using the platform, the more value you're getting out of the platform. In reality, it's not that simple or straightforward. Vendors are notoriously bad at understanding your workflow and how their technology and all its features affect your product for better or worse. They focus on working with clients to maximize feature usage rather than business value. In reality, they may be encouraging a customer to use features that don't improve workflow at all and may be hindering it, creating more work for people and ultimately having an adverse effect on the product, departmental objectives, and business goals. That isn't what they're thinking about, though—they want you to use everything they have to offer so you're dependent on it and more likely to renew.

The typical SaaS vendor's priority is velocity. A SaaS company that sells HR software doesn't hire salespeople who know about HR or software or how to sell to people who buy it. The company hires sales reps who excel at velocity. *How fast can I get you signed up? How many features can I throw at you?* Once you're sold, the customer success team takes over and tries to get you to use all the features so you're more likely to renew everything. This sales approach plays right into the "too much tech, not enough strategy" problem. You want a quick fix for a problem or for a symptom of the problem, and the vendor is right there with a solution, ready to close the deal.

The pressure on decision-makers to buy the tech and use the features is real. It's not uncommon for us to be on a call with a client who has a vendor present while we discuss departmental initiatives that support company objectives. The vendors' comments are seldom around business goals. More often, there are numerous interjections of "You should use our technology for that" and "Is our technology going to be used?" and "How can we get our solution into that?" It's usually all about them and what they have, instead of about the client and their goals. The pressure's on during the sales process, and once a purchase is made, the vendor engages further, often continuing the pressure. They are not happy until they're fully entrenched with a stranglehold on the company and how it operates.

Tech buyers readily give in to the pressure. When a vendor makes their solution sound like the perfect solution, you want it because you want your problems to go away. You want everything to work the way the vendor says it will, and you are attracted to the thought of having someone to blame—the vendor—if it doesn't. Unfortunately, their solution isn't always the best solution or even the right solution for your needs. If you're in the market for cloud software, vendors will tell you their cloud does everything, and it's predesigned to integrate with all your other software, and of course it's the best because this industry leader, and this one, and that one over there are all using it. You want to believe. You really do. You want to hand the whole mess off to one vendor so you have just one company to blame if it all falls apart. That's better than the alternative—having many companies to blame and all of them pointing fingers at each other. So you buy the thing, and you have one vendor and one invoice. Whether the cloud—or any other technology—you purchased actually makes sense for your business is kind of an afterthought.

BUYING TECH: THE GO-TO SOLUTION FOR BUSINESS PROBLEMS

Without a holistic view of customer experience technology and the departments that support it, visibility into the actual problems is limited. You could probably solve the problem if you knew what it was, but each department sees only the symptoms. Doing something feels better than doing nothing, so you try to solve for the symptom, often by adding more technology.

I'm a hammer. You must be a nail!

—OUR INTERPRETATION OF MASLOW'S HAMMER IN ACTION IN MANY ORGANIZATIONS

For example, say you aren't getting the conversions you expect from the forms on your website. To remedy the issue, you install a chatbot. The chatbot is supposed to solve the conversion problem by engaging customers, but you can't really know whether it addresses the problem or not because you are treating the symptom. Customers may be having problems with the website that have nothing to do with the forms. Maybe they can't even find the forms. Without due diligence to discover the true problem that's causing low conversion rates, you have no reason to get your hopes up over the chatbot.

In businesses with multiple divisions, geographic locations, and product lines, with multiple teams that have overlapping responsibilities, the issue is compounded. Each individual team wants to solve their symptom, but no one sees the big problem. So you end up with many solutions, none of them work together, and none of them solve the problem. That is a big, expensive, avoidable mistake.

To make matters worse, the decision-makers in these purchases are usually compensated for meeting their department's objectives. They have no motivation to purchase technology that makes another department's job easier or their odds of success better. And everyone's on a tight timeline, so even if they could talk to each other, no one at the top sees the value in actually collaborating, so they aren't given the time.

TECHNOLOGY HAS ITS OWN TECHNOLOGY

Often, when you buy a tool or a platform, you later realize there are various add-ons. These add-ons may come from the vendor, or they may be from a third party. They fill in feature gaps or process gaps to simplify a particular workflow within the product and enhance its overall capability. Some tech has a veritable ecosystem of add-ons, which creates a multiplier effect around the technology usage and complexity. From an administrative and a maintenance standpoint, you might think you're buying one technology from one vendor, but really, you could have five technologies from several vendors—even though you purchased the tech from one company—and that increases the burden of management and oversight.

When you look at data security and accessibility, the problem of technology having its own technology is especially troubling. For example, a third-party technology that has access to your data could be collecting that data. Unless you're a technology expert, you may not be aware that's happening. Marketers shouldn't have to worry about this—they should be focused on becoming experts on using technology to solve their business problems.

NO ONE IS TRACKING OR OWNING THE TECH

Security issues caused by a lack of knowledge transfer are more common than you would think. Someone buys a tool for a specific purpose and maintains that tool, but then they leave. This creates a knowledge gap: no one knows what the tech does, how many add-on tools it has, or how any of it works.

And unless the technology had executive sponsorship at the time of purchase, it may not even be used again. This is less likely to happen if the technology had executive sponsorship at the time of purchase, but that's not always the case. More often, someone in the department needs a tool, they get the tool and use the tool, and when they leave, no one ever touches it again. If the technology was purchased to support a business goal, it's more likely that there would be visibility from a higher level in the company—at the department level or higher.

If the technology isn't tracked across the organization, people who need it may not have access—or even know it exists. During a client health check, we interviewed all the stakeholders around a project.

We asked one team, "How do you organize and manage your projects?"

"Well, everybody just sort of does their own thing," we were told. "We could really use a project management system, though." They named one they had their eye on, but it wasn't in the budget.

Later that day, we posed the same question to another team.

They told us, "We have a terrific project management system—everyone loves it!"

You guessed it: this team already owned the system the other team wanted. All they had to do was buy more seats, and they could all be working in the same system.

In another interview, we discovered that one person was using two tools to manage all the business's social media.

GOING ROGUE

Sales Ops and Marketing Ops didn't always exist. They evolved when they couldn't get the technology or services they needed from IT. Yet, expecting IT to deal with Marketing Ops, Sales Ops, and other tech owners isn't efficient. It's also not fair to those CX support people, who have responsibility but often lack the technical expertise necessary to manage a project without asking for IT's help, or who are on a tight deadline and can't wait for IT to respond to a request for access or permission to do something. CX tech groups may bypass IT's authority by "going rogue," but shadow IT groups are not the solution.

These teams had good intentions, but with no oversight, they were basically shadow IT groups buying technology that didn't always play well with existing tech. When things started to go wrong, the shadow IT team didn't know what to do, and the IT department didn't want to deal with the problem. Eventually, these Ops teams were formalized, but there still exists a disconnect between them, IT, and other Ops teams.

A company we worked with took shadow IT to the extreme. One marketing team purchased and installed a SaaS platform, and other teams followed suit. The individual teams split the payments, so the invoices were never big enough to warrant signing authority at a level that would have attracted attention. By the time IT was aware of the install, eleven databases across North America were running the rogue platform. This wasn't started by a few people in the lower ranks—a marketing VP, tired of waiting for an indecisive CMO to act, made the decision and the initial purchase.

When the time came to renew the contract for the company's IT-installed system, the vendor noted a considerable drop in usage over the past couple of years. In fact, the platform wasn't being used at all. The jig was up.

How no one outside of this rogue group—which at this point was a majority of Marketing—noticed the drastic decline in usage over a period of time is anyone's guess. But the incident makes you wonder how often similar situations play out in businesses around the world.

The problem was that no one else knew anything about these tools. If the woman suddenly went away, the company's social media channels would come to an abrupt halt.

Businesses have tech that no one tracks. They have tech that no one owns. They have tech that isn't being used, and they want and need tech that they already own. When there's a merger or an acquisition, the problems are compounded.

Some organizations are incredibly good at tracking tech, inventorying it regularly, and determining what to keep and what to toss. But too often, unused technology is forgotten. Eventually, the contracts expire.

Buying authority comes with great responsibility. When you purchase blindly with no strategy, you're going to pay more upfront, and you're going to keep paying for it. If you do get to a point where you're ready to manage the tech holistically to meet company goals, you will have a lot to sort through. Some of the tech might work together, and some will not. There might be dependencies between tools that you don't know about. You might have multiple tools that do the same thing. Having a plan for the tech—what it's going to do for you and how it's going to work with what you have—is the first step in preventing a massive technology graveyard.

Have you seen the movie *Up in the Air*? The George Clooney character has a scene where he's talking about putting everything that's weighing you down in a backpack. Imagine putting all the tech that you're trying to manage in a pack and carrying it around the office. How does that feel? Exhausting, right? That's exactly what it's like to have too much tech and not enough strategy—like a heavy backpack, weighing you down and sapping all your energy.

Martech budgets could be facing budgetary pressure for another reason: CMOs struggle to effectively manage their marketing technology stack. Almost a quarter (24%) of Gartner's 2019 Marketing Organization Survey respondents said that marketing technology strategy, adoption and use is one of their top three weaknesses in their company's ability to drive customer acquisition or loyalty. More than 25% blamed weaknesses in their martech strategy on insufficient budget, resources or capabilities.[6]

---

6   Ewan McIntyre and Anna Maria Virzi, "CMO Spend Survey 2019-2020: CMOs Double Down on Digital Channels and Analytics, but Fail to Plan for Tough Times Ahead," *Gartner for Marketers*, 2020, https://emtemp.gcom.cloud/ngw/globalassets/en/marketing/documents/annual-cmo-spend-survey-research.pdf.

IF YOU ONLY KNEW WHAT YOU HAD

During a certification training, the instructor was talking about how to re-engage customers who go dark, which is a point of accountability for customer success managers. Half the people in the room were in that role, so their ears perked up. The instructor said that you first need to understand *why* they're not responding to you. Are they engaged with someone else in your organization? Are they out of the office and traveling for work or on vacation? You have to know this so you're not just pestering them with phone calls and emails.

We had been doing some consulting work for the company where seven of these customer success managers worked, but we weren't working with these people on this team, so we had never met. They began talking among themselves about what the instructor was saying.

"We really need to do this," one of them said. "Yes," said another, "I wish I had a way to know whether my emails were read. If only we had more visibility into how people were engaging with us."

They talked about tools they had used in the past to solve these problems, mulling over why they didn't have the technology they needed at their current company. The consensus was that they had a major problem and would have to convince their bosses to buy some new tech to help them out.

Because we were engaged with another team at their business, we knew they already had this technology. The company just hadn't purchased licenses for the full functionality of the product. Of course, we had to clue them in. We introduced ourselves and told them the news.

"You have the solution. You just need licenses. Here's the name of your administrator who can help you out." If we hadn't, they would have made the same mistake so many teams make when they don't have access, visibility, or even knowledge of technology installed at their own company.

A BETTER VIEW

Do you know what kind of tools other departments have? Do you know how those tools interact with your customers? Do they know what you have? Imagine if someone has visibility into all of that—a high-level view of all the tech and how it's affecting the customer experience.

The tendency to buy tech to solve a problem—without knowing the real problem—happens in every department. If you polled the department heads, they would probably all tell you they have the same issue. The bigger problem is that no one has a plan for fixing it. There are too many barriers in place for any single person or department to lead the charge. These organizational barriers are partially responsible for the problem, but the issue of too much tech without a holistic strategy also puts up more barriers. Do you want to know what other people are using? Are you ready to accept that knowledge and potentially the responsibility of doing something about it?

This gets to the heart of the matter: the relationships that develop between departments and how the traditional structure hinders collaboration, alignment, and growth. The lack of transparency creates a dysfunctional company, and like a dysfunctional relationship, someone has to step outside their comfort zone and take responsibility for not only their pains but the illness that has taken over the whole organization. This does not happen often enough.

CHAPTER 4

NOT MY MONKEYS, NOT MY CIRCUS

There comes a time when one must take a position that is neither safe, nor politic, nor popular, but he must take it because conscience tells him it is right.

—MARTIN LUTHER KING, JR.

Mike was at an extracurricular activity with his daughter last year. The parents sat in a waiting room while their children finished their lessons. It was winter, and coats, hats, and gloves hung on hooks on the wall. Mike waited with his daughter on his lap in the crowded room. There was a hat in the middle of the floor. People crossed the room going in and out, taking care not to step on the hat. But the hat lay there, untouched, because no one wanted to take responsibility for it.

The hat obviously belonged to someone. It was getting dirty there on the floor and in danger of being trampled. Someone could have tripped over it. Mike watched the people avoid it for a while before getting out of his chair, picking up the hat, and hanging it on a hook.

This is normal human behavior, and it's as common in the workplace as it is in a waiting room. Nobody wants to touch someone else's problem. They haven't been assigned responsibility, and no one's asked them to help, so even though they clearly see it, they politely step over it or look the other way.

NOT MY HAT, NOT MY PROBLEM

The "not my monkeys, not my circus" (or in this example, "not my hat, not my problem") issue pervades business and is exacerbated not only because most people don't *want* the responsibility—they're often prevented from even *seeing* it due to barriers that exist in the typical workplace.

A traditionally organized business does not encourage collaboration—the structure practically prevents it. People might see what they perceive as a problem in another department or function, but without visibility into that function, they assume that maybe it's not a problem at all, but that they just don't understand it. In other words: they see the hat, shrug, and think, "Yeah, there's a hat on the floor. Guess it's supposed to be there, or surely someone else would have picked it up!"

In business, the impact trickles down to the customer. People often don't want to address the inherent limitations that prevent them from doing their best work. For example, you might have two marketing managers whose objectives overlap: one's focus is marketing a particular widget ten different ways, and the other's is marketing all the widgets one way. So one widget is being marketed in different ways by different managers and their teams. Sales is selling these widgets, and since they're typically talking to just one of the marketing teams, yet their marketing collateral might come from another team, the collateral they provide to their customers may not align with what they're actually telling them.

These barriers manifest themselves within processes that affect project outcomes too. For instance, Marketing might need Sales' input on a project, but the data they're getting from Sales is incomplete, and what they do get is questionable. Everyone on the marketing team knows this is a problem. Yet no one is willing to do anything about it because Sales has their directives for gathering data and Marketing has theirs. The salespeople gather only the data that *their* manager wants them to gather—data that helps Sales' objectives. So instead of working together toward a process that benefits both groups and, ultimately, the company's goals, they work around each other.

In a company, problems like these are more serious than a hat on the floor. They are the proverbial "elephant in the room" that everyone tiptoes around. If someone would stand up and say, "Hey, look at that elephant! Let's do something about that beast," then maybe other people would acknowledge it and begin to deal with it. And they should. Because that elephant isn't just getting in the way—it's crushing the business.

POLITICS (AS USUAL)

Interdepartmental politics are another reason for ignoring problems. No one wants to "step in it" because just dealing with other people and their problems is exhausting. Subconsciously or intentionally, people put blinders on and march ahead. As long as they focus on what's in front of them, it's easier to ignore other people's chaos. That way, they don't have to deal with anything that takes attention away from what they're trying to accomplish. As long as they don't acknowledge a problem, they don't have to own it. It's somebody else's monkey, someone else's circus.

Even if they do believe there's a problem, politics can prevent people from speaking up. No one wants to be the one to say something and embarrass themselves because they're wrong or risk offending someone because they're right. It's not their place to point out problems—it isn't *anyone's* place. And the first person to speak up probably isn't going to be very popular around the office. The barriers between departments can become personal barriers, and people usually don't want to cross those.

Rather than step on toes and create a situation, people resort to workarounds that are often more labor intensive and deliver suboptimal results. It's easier to work within your department and avoid those additional conversations, the risk of stirring up conflict, and possibly getting your plans derailed. When presented with two options, most people will pick the one that comes with the fewest headaches, especially busy people who don't want to rock the boat and just want to get the job done.

Avoiding requests for collaboration between departments is all too common. There's usually a history behind the situation, like earlier requests made and not answered. Departments might accept a request and commit resources to it, but because it's not a priority for them, the request gets shifted around with no real progress. The people responsible move on to other projects, and six months later, nothing's been done, and the requester basically gives up—and makes a mental note to avoid projects that require collaboration. Why bother asking for things you know you will never have?

USE YOUR WORDS

As parents, we teach our children to "use their words." Speaking up is the best way to express their wishes and make sure they're heard and clearly understood. Many adults seem to lose that skill in the workplace.

A marketing team we worked with was building a nurture campaign. At a point in the process, leads needed to go to the lead development rep (LDR), who would qualify them before sending the leads to Sales. The goal was to create a process where a prospect's actions drove leads directly to the LDR with no human intervention. The results of the LDR's attempts to reach the individual then drove the next actions in the campaign. Working with the LDR, we devised a seamless process that would be invaluable in their revenue generation efforts.

To fully automate the process, we needed to add two fields to the lead record and populate them with data points. One would direct the LDR to the right script for reaching out, and the other would disposition the call properly to trigger the associated email campaign. This would be an easy task for the CRM administrator.

Except that our client, the marketing manager, did not own the CRM. It was owned by Sales Ops. When we sensed some hesitancy from our client on this step in the plan, we asked him why. It turned out there was a lot of tension between the departments, and our client eventually said, "We do not want to have that conversation. Tell us how we make this happen without Sales Ops' help."

Because of the client's reluctance to make that simple request to Sales Ops, we had to create a workaround that pulled in data from other sources, populated the right fields, and triggered the right events. Despite that "success," the workaround necessitated manual intervention from the LDR that would have been avoided with the fully automated process we had originally proposed and could have easily delivered. From discovery to build to test and launch, that workaround took *sixty hours* to create. All that extra time, effort, and *money* for a problem that could have been solved in minutes with a simple request: "Hey Sales Ops, we need you to add these two fields on the lead record in the CRM."

People know this behavior goes on, but no one acknowledges it. In many workplaces, it's how work gets done—or *not* done—with each person focused on their primary responsibilities, seldom asking for help or offering to help anyone else.

STRATEGIC PLANNING IS OFTEN INEFFECTIVE

Companies usually take one of two approaches to planning: either far in advance or not at all.

The old-school way of strategic planning usually begins in the fourth quarter of the company's fiscal year, where individuals, teams, and departments develop a plan for the next year. Budget is typically tied to that plan, with estimates of what it will cost and the expected return. Those plans are put in front of whoever controls the budget, and that person approves or disapproves the plan or asks the planner to adjust their respective plan. Then the person, team, or department gets their budget for the next year.

The challenge with old-school strategic planning is that

business moves so fast that those plans become irrelevant quickly. People need to pivot to accommodate a new situation, meet a new challenge, or take advantage of a new opportunity. But because the budget's earmarked for a project they proposed months ago, they're constrained to *that* plan and proceed with it whether it makes sense for the business or not.

Today, a lot of companies have given up trying to plan ahead, knowing their business situation will change. Instead of following a fourth-quarter planning period, they don't plan at all. They commit resources to an initiative and move on to the next initiative that pops up. But if there is no strategy involved to connect these initiatives, people gravitate toward projects that support what's already working. In marketing, if demand generation is successful, they throw more resources at demand generation. If nurturing leads or social media marketing is working, they spend more time and money on initiatives around nurture and social media. So much for innovation. So much for improving the weakest links in a company's processes. And so much for taking a holistic approach to improving the customer experience and generating revenue.

The marketing leader who values planning but doesn't have a way to pivot from an established plan is still limited. The leader who doesn't plan—instead launching one project after another aimed at what the department's already doing well—ignores the opportunities and doesn't address the challenges. Neither approach is effective.

Sticking to an out-of-date plan come hell or high water doesn't make sense. Neither does throwing more time and money at the same tired old plans without considering what *could* be with some better planning, a little imagination, and the guts to take a few risks.

Marketing professionals don't intentionally sabotage their projects. Poor planning is usually due to a lack of time. There is just too much to do. Those who can find time to plan recognize that the buying landscape and technology that supports it are changing so fast that trying to stay current feels like a lost cause. They believe that by the time they come up with a decent plan, it will likely be outdated.

In recent years, the situation has gotten worse to the point where many marketers have practically given up on planning. They want to plan. They wish they could, with some certainty that their plans would make sense in three months. But they can't.

Barriers between departments and company politics also play a role in planning, especially when a leader's plan involves departments under another leader's control. As one marketing manager told us, "We have a plan, but it's irrelevant." She was trying to build an evergreen campaign to promote ongoing engagement, but her team didn't own the content. It was owned by the content team. If she did manage to get the content and launch the program, since she did not manage the sales team, there was no guarantee that any leads generated by the campaign would receive follow-up.

"I'm hesitant to publicly commit to a project being done well or to any results because my influence is so limited," she said.

These two approaches to planning—meticulous yet set in stone and no planning at all—are common but not the rule, even within a company. Some businesses might have a few marketing teams that plan very well and can pivot as they roll out their plans, yet they have to interact with many other departments that haven't yet figured it out.

This situation shouldn't be surprising. Look at what Marketing has to deal with: a massive amount of digital, omnichannel communication to every customer a business is trying to reach. While responsible for it, they don't have authority over all of it. It's impossible to make a plan and commit to an outcome when you don't have control over all the parts and pieces that contribute to that outcome. Is it any wonder marketing leaders are reluctant to plan and unable to do so with any degree of certainty?

LITTLE OR NO ANALYSIS

Exacerbating the problem is a lack of analysis. Plans are made without first examining the data that's available and analyzing it to inform decisions around planning. Automated data collection provides the numbers: deliverability, opens, clicks, and other calls to action (CTA), such as registrations. However, analyzing those numbers to identify trends and patterns is typically *not* automated, and it's not a high enough priority for anyone to find the time to do it. And when the analysis *is* done, it's usually within an initiative or campaign rather than across all of marketing because that takes more time.

Some of this lack of analysis is due to a disconnect between systems within a department or between different departments. You might have access to data from one system but not another, or the data may be presented differently between systems, and no one's figured out how to normalize it. Without a data team specifically assigned to analysis, that work is seldom done, which leads to inferior project planning. When a project ends, unless there's a concerted effort to examine the results, any potential marketing intelligence is wasted. Though vanity metrics like views and clicks are considered, true KPIs that impact the customer experience and revenue aren't analyzed, and the intelligence isn't incorporated into future campaigns.

LACK OF PROCESS CONSISTENCY AND OWNERSHIP

At many companies, processes aren't always mapped out. They aren't documented and communicated. You might think everyone completes a task the same way, but chances are they do not. Some follow a process that's been shared informally among the team. Others do it their own way. And no one's accountable for the process—who does it, the steps to follow, or the reason it even exists.

This isn't always true across an organization. One team may be super organized with a knowledge management system or shared documentation, so everyone knows what to do and how to do it. The team next to them, though, is winging it. They think they don't have time to create processes or even put someone in charge of them.

Silos play a role in this issue too, because people could be sitting in the same room doing basically the same job, but since they're in different departments that don't talk openly, one has the luxury of an expedient process while the other makes it up as they go. The barriers that exist not only affect the company, they again trickle down to the customer.

For example, let's look at a business that does events for other companies. The salesperson sells the event to a client, then engages the content team to develop the event's content. That team is responsible for writing emails, creating landing pages, and developing other collateral that's tailored to the customer. They need certain information about the client, and since that relationship is owned by the salesperson (who is essentially now the account manager), they rely on that person to get it.

This works fine if Sales has a good process for getting the right information. Too often, there is no process. The salesperson sells the event their way, makes commitments to the customer, and gathers what they think they need to make the sale. Some sales departments or salespeople might have a process that meshes very well with what the content team needs to do their job well, while others—well, not so much.

The content team settles for whatever they get and does the best they can with it, and then they pass it to Marketing for execution. No one owns the processes within Sales or Marketing, and no one owns the entire process end-to-end, so the quality of the event varies dramatically depending on which salesperson sells the event.

You're probably thinking, "Why doesn't Marketing tell the content team what they need from them to execute? Why doesn't the content team tell Sales what they need to create high-quality content?"

Again, people are reluctant to have those conversations. The quality of the event suffers, the teams suffer because they can't do their best work, and the customer suffers, too, because they don't get what they expected.

If there is tension between departments, that reluctance is understandable. But too often, the problem could be solved if someone simply asked, "Hey, how about we get on the same page about this process?" This doesn't have to be a formal email or meeting, and in fact, it's better if it isn't. There doesn't have to be pressure—a person can just walk up to another person in their office or in the hallway or message them on Slack. Anyone can ask the question and start the conversation. The worst-case response is likely to be, "We like our process and don't want to change it." At least then a person knows what they're up against. Usually, the conversation never happens because, again, people are reluctant to cross those invisible barriers that divide people, teams, functions, and departments. Everyone settles for a disjointed, uneven collection of processes that lead to an inferior product and, often, an unhappy customer.

WHY DO I HAVE TO BE THE RINGMASTER?

By now, you're probably worn out just reading this. One problem after another—too many hats on the floor, elephants in the room, and monkeys in the circus. But now you can see them, in this chapter and maybe in your own company.

The first major problem that looms over many businesses is a lack of transparency. It creates impenetrable silos between each department's people, technology, and processes. This leads to the second problem: each silo has its own people, tech, and processes, creating a complex and often incongruent customer experience. These two problems could be solved if it weren't for the third one: a lack of courage. Until someone steps up to pick up the hat, call out the elephant, and own those monkeys, the other two problems will always exist.

At this point, you may be thinking, "Why do I have to be the ringmaster?" You have enough to do. Why should you be the one to go out on a limb and own all those problems? Why should you even *care*? Since you're still reading, we have a hunch that you do care. You care *a lot*. And you recognize the enormous opportunity that's presented itself. You just need a little guidance.

We see these problems at companies every day, and we help people take them on. The results show us that one person can make a huge difference, and they show us what's possible. We're going to talk about all that—what you can do, and how to do it—but first let's talk about *why* you should bother in the first place. Why it all matters.

CHAPTER 5

WHY IT ALL MATTERS

A ship in harbor is safe, but that's not what ships are built for.

—JOHN AUGUSTUS SHEDD

Imagine logging onto a company's site and going back and forth with a chatbot for twenty minutes, then being told that a salesperson will be reaching out to you to address your request. The next day, you get a phone call, but the salesperson evidently has none of the information you provided to the chatbot. Do they expect you to repeat everything all over again? Your time is valuable, and that company just wasted it. Do they really want your business? Yet that's what businesses subject customers to *every single day*. The technology is in place to prevent these miscommunications; it's just not implemented properly.

Prospects and clients don't reach out to a sales department

or marketing department. They connect to businesses digitally. Who they connect with, the information they provide, and what they see and hear is up to the business, and how its technology is structured and digital content is delivered. A reluctance to acknowledge that fact and make sure they're getting the right message out costs companies money—and customers.

Twenty years ago, companies realized that technology was the way of the future. The future is now, and the technology is here. And while businesses have invested in it, they struggle to implement technology in a way that leverages all it has to offer. It's like giving up a landline for a cell phone, then tethering the cell to your desk so you can't use it anywhere else. Technology allows us to organize functions, people, and processes in a way that's free of physical limitations. Yet, many companies are still organized like landlines in a cell phone world.

CONSISTENCY COUNTS

When you talk to a friend or a coworker, it's not like you're seeing them for the first time. You know them, and you're continuing the ongoing conversation you have with them. That's what great B2C businesses do, and it's what your B2B customers want from you. This is about consistency. It's about interacting with people *within the context of all the information they've already provided to you.* Those interactions should have continuity—just like any other relationship. The closer you can get to this, the better the customer experience will be. Ultimately, we're talking about relationship marketing because buying isn't a one-shot deal. From attracting a prospect to providing support to a repeat customer, a lot happens in between that either creates a relationship—or doesn't.

[Among B2B buyers], 66% expect their interactions with vendors to be personalized, versus 56% of B2C buyers...84% of marketers say they actively listen, act on feedback, and close the feedback loop, while only 69% of B2B buyers feel this is true of the vendors they interact with.[7]

CUSTOMERS WANT SOMETHING BACK

Within these interactions, businesses ask customers for information. People who give up information about themselves expect something in return. They want to know what companies do with the data: Does it disappear into a black hole? Or is it helping the business track the customer's browsing behavior on the company's website? Is that information being leveraged to improve the customer experience and benefit the customer? The expectation may not be explicitly stated, but it's there, even subconsciously, in

---

7   Emily Sue Tomac, "The Engagement Economy: How to build the relationship B2B buyers want," TrustRadius.com, October 13, 2017, https://www.trustradius.com/vendor-blog/engagement-economy-how-to-build-the-relationship-b2b-buyers-want.

the mind of the customer. Siloed organizations with disconnected departments and discrete data are unable to deliver value in return for information because they don't have a collective body of information from the various omnichannel points of contact.

One reason consumer, versus B2B, businesses often do this so well is that transactions between them and their customers are self-contained. They gather information, make the sale, follow up, and repeat. A click ad on Instagram that's tailored to the customer based on their browsing behavior leads to a purchase, providing the company with information confirming their belief that yes, the customer does indeed like shirts made from a particular material that's soft and doesn't need ironing. Within minutes, the buyer has a great experience. It's not hindered or delayed by long, drawn-out processes within the company: getting company buy-in and budget, and polling all the decision-makers, and making sure the shirt matches everyone else's pants. The seller doesn't have to worry about connecting the dots between campaigns, responses to the campaigns, and transactions by the point of contact or someone at their organization. It's just not that complicated. Companies buying from other companies is a lot harder, and it's difficult to maintain consistency over time.

IT'S GOING TO GET HARDER

Businesses are in a continuous cycle of launching new products, buying competitors, and taking other actions that rely on increasingly complex but often disparate customer interactions. At this point in the evolution of revenue, functions like Sales, Marketing, Service, and Support (which, for the sake of brevity, we'll refer to as the CX teams for now) are touching the customer, and if companies don't get a handle on those interactions, sales will disappear. By the way, your CX teams may comprise more or fewer departments, and they may have different names. As long as they directly impact the customer experience, they fall within that grouping and are part of the discussion.

Whatever changes are at hand, companies have to continue communicating with stakeholders, customers, partners, and vendors. That communication tends to go through Marketing. If you're running your CX teams separately with no holistic vision or structure for that communication, you will not survive.

You can narrow the output funnel, but that means narrowing the top to compensate. As long as you see your departments separately, your business growth will be limited. Marketing is your best bet for bringing all the departments together to communicate a consistent message to everyone. If you don't, your business can stagnate and then decline.

We see companies make this fatal mistake all the time. Businesses that fail to provide consistent, cohesive messaging may not see the decline immediately because customers will hang in there patiently, waiting for a turnaround or for something better to come along. It won't happen overnight, but little by little the competition chips away at their business, and one by one their customers disappear. A major reason so many companies don't change is that they don't see the end coming until it's too late. By the time they realize they need to change how they interact with customers, they're gasping for air with little hope for survival. Meanwhile, other businesses have moved in to disrupt them—agile ones that have figured this whole tech and revenue thing out. Eventually, the company that doesn't change hits a threshold—a sort of point of no return. Fresh ideas dry up, innovation declines, and the best employees find a better place to work.

GOOD PEOPLE LEAVE

A stagnating business leads to dwindling employee satisfaction and increased turnover. The best people leave, while the mediocre ones stay. Productive and talented people who bring enthusiasm and intensity to their work do not stick around in a place where problems are met with lackadaisical responses. In time, the workplace actually *attracts* people who don't care about growing the business but are just there to do a job.

LOSS OF INNOVATION

If the stagnant business happens to land a creative super-star, that person gets locked into dealing with the mundane, day-to-day issues, and they never get a chance to innovate. The pressure to take care of daily tasks and get the work done—basically, do what gets measured—takes away any incentive to come up with new ideas. Where innovation isn't valued, it languishes, and that can be a death sentence for a business trying to grow.

SILOED BUSINESS, SILOED IDEAS

In a siloed organization, information and ideas are siloed. Instead of taking advantage of the collective expertise of people from different departments, employees sink into a kind of groupthink among their closest coworkers. When they stop sharing knowledge and thoughts, a sort of arti-ficial suppression occurs, and people stop coming up with original ideas. People may change what's visible to them and within their influence, but the benefits of collabora-tion and sharing of ideas are lost. Without communication, interaction, and collaboration between departments, the opportunity for a greater understanding and better decision-making isn't possible.

NO MOMENTUM, NO VELOCITY

Velocity is a measurement of how fast the business moves

in a particular direction to achieve a certain magnitude of change. Speed will get you somewhere fast, but you need a direction that takes you to substantial changes to achieve velocity. To have velocity, you need a goal, direction to that goal, and momentum to move toward that goal quickly. A single momentum gain or ones created by individual departments don't cut it. Continuous momentum "boosts" that move the business forward are needed to achieve substantial velocity, and that isn't possible in a siloed company.

Amazon is a great example of momentum versus velocity. The company launched in 1994, IPOed three years later in '97, and expanded beyond books the following year. From 1998 to 2004, they made incremental progress and had momentum but no real velocity. In 2005, with the launch of Amazon Prime, the company progressed to a whole new order of magnitude. Next came Amazon Web Services in 2006, then Amazon Music, AmazonFresh, and Kindle in 2007, acquiring Zappos in 2009, launching AppStore in 2011, acquiring Whole Foods in 2017, and a velocity that allowed them to become the behemoth they are today, dominating entire industries.

Velocity isn't exactly a goal—it's more an environment that's created by taking down the barriers that hold you back. Velocity derives its power from many forces traveling in the same direction. Removing the barriers to that movement makes velocity possible. Imagine a busy city street where cars are moving in different directions. Even if you're going as fast as you can in the right direction, you're going to be held back by all those other cars. They're like speedbumps preventing you from getting any momentum.

Now, compare that with a street where cars are all moving in the same direction. The drivers will naturally increase their speeds to match the fastest driver, and everyone will reach their destination more quickly. A siloed organization doesn't allow people to benefit from others' progress or momentum, and it doesn't allow for the kind of innovation that drives velocity.

Moving a business to a state of velocity isn't an easy task, though—it takes courage to force yourself to look beyond your own department. You have to choose a direction everyone will go. Then everyone has to stop focusing on momentum that brings just their department forward and start focusing on what creates velocity for the entire company.

MORE THAN ALIGNMENT

Although aligning goals is a part of the solution, it's not the whole solution (despite what your friendly neighborhood alignment consultant will have you believe). Too much has changed for a simple alignment of goals to bring about the kind of shift companies must make to avoid—*continuing the car analogy*—getting stuck in bumper-to-bumper traffic.

Most companies are trying to make do with what they have rather than lining up behind the revenue and getting growth out of it. You can be like them, or you can be a company that lines up behind the revenue—and lasts, thrives, and keeps growing. The company every other company is looking out for and struggling to get ahead of. Without a major change, companies that don't get behind the revenue suffer the consequences. If you're not first in revenue velocity, you might as well be last.

THERE IS A BETTER WAY

I have no desire to suffer twice, in reality and then in retrospect.

—SOPHOCLES, *OEDIPUS REX*

Giving these problems the attention they deserve does more than save your business from all the negative fallout. Solving them has enormous benefits. It makes you a brutal opponent among your competitors. Your prospects will become customers, and your customers will come back for more. Your employees will stay, knowing they're valued and contributing to the company's success instead of being a cog in the wheel. Your company can experience exponential growth, and people will want to be a part of that. They'll be drawn to it. While other businesses stagnate and shrink, you'll be moving forward and growing.

WHAT IF I DON'T WANT TO GROW MY BUSINESS?

We knew that would get your attention. Of course, *you* want to grow your business. That doesn't mean *everyone* at your company wants it to grow. Sometimes company leaders or investors have different goals, like cutting costs and making as much profit as possible in the short term. They may be preparing to divest assets or leverage the business in other ways to make it more attractive to a potential buyer. Leaders with initiatives like these aren't likely to share that information with everyone in the company—even their own colleagues. If you're getting a lot of pushback on growth or you feel like your leader is working against you and you don't know why, they may be focused on *non-growth* activities. A reluctance to improve infrastructure or make the kinds of changes that can bring about massive growth may be a signal that there are discussions happening behind the scenes that you're not privy to. If this sounds familiar, address your concerns with leadership and listen to their response. You need to know where you stand and where the company stands before you put a lot of effort into a business that's on a different trajectory than the one you think it's on.

HOW HARD IS THIS GOING TO BE?

The shift from traditional structure to Revenue Takeover—with all CX teams collaborating under one umbrella to drive revenue—can be as hard or as easy as a company wants to make it. New businesses that haven't settled into an immovable structure tend to have the agility, ability, and willingness to adopt this change quickly. Surprisingly, some mature companies are also great candidates for a Revenue Takeover because they've been through big changes before. When you propose a shift in direction, people's heads don't spin around. They know that markets change, tech changes, and customers' needs change and that they've had to make changes over the years to remain viable. This is not true for all new or older businesses, though, and much depends on leadership and company culture. For some, change is part of the culture, and they welcome a pivot or a restructure. The key to making the shift from a traditional structure to one that supports a Revenue Takeover is strong leadership that embraces change and a culture that thrives in a dynamic environment.

THE PATH TO GREATNESS

All of these problems may seem insurmountable. You may be thinking, "Why bother?" In a word: *Greatness*. Greatness awaits the marketing leader who sees and seizes the opportunity these problems present and the Revenue Takeover that changes how people think, operate, and do business in this new buying landscape. Sure, it's going to be hard. Of course it's complicated. But we're giving you the playbook to get it done. You have the know-how. You probably have the motivation, too. If you're struggling with that, think back on why you got into business in the first place. Think about how exciting it is when everything goes right, and you can trace the business's growth and revenue directly back to the contributions of all the people who showed up to go the extra mile and make a difference. You're smart enough to do this. The question is: are you brave enough?

One step at a time, one courageous act at a time, and you will get there. We'll step you through it in phases.

If you're at this point in the book and none of these problems resonate, kudos to you. You probably don't need to read any further. But if you're experiencing any of these struggles, they are holding you back from greatness and hindering you from fulfilling your organization's goals. In that case, keep reading. The future is next, and it's yours if you want it.

.

PART II

THE FUTURE

Imagine a future where your B2B customer experience is seamless. Marketing, Sales, Support, and Success are all working together to deliver an optimized experience. The metrics and goals of these teams are aligned under a holistic strategy, and they're supported by a centralized revenue operations team. You are leaving the competition in the dust—and beating the company's revenue goals! Let's see what that looks like.

CHAPTER 6

IF IT ISN'T WORKING FOR THE CUSTOMER, IT ISN'T WORKING

Just because something is traditional is no reason to do it, of course.

—LEMONY SNICKET

Of all the companies we've relied on for products, one was flawless. Our orders arrived intact, on time, every time. We never had to return anything. After years of weekly purchases from the company, one day they sent us a faulty product.

At first, we didn't know what to do, but we knew we weren't excited about it. None of us wanted to deal with what we *expected* to happen—phone calls, long waits on hold, being transferred from one person to the next, and endless questions about how the product got broken in the first place.

We went to their website. All our orders were listed, and it only took a few seconds to find the product. From there, we went straight into a sort of AI chat that walked us through a decision tree:

Is there a problem with the order? Yes.

Can you explain the problem? It's broken.

Do you want a replacement product, a refund, or a credit? Credit.

Okay, would you like to return the product by mailing it to us, or would you like us to pick it up, or would you prefer to drop it off at your nearest drop-off location?

We chose to drop it off since that was easiest. All we had to do was put the product back in the box and bring it to our nearest location along with the return number they provided. That was it. No phone calls, hold times, or explanations. No messing around with the packaging or waiting for a pick-up. We didn't even have to bother with a packing slip. They took care of everything. It was the most seamless experience we've had with a company ever, or since.

They valued our business, or at least that's how we felt. They didn't make us jump through hoops or expend any energy or waste any time over the problem—they never even broke our rhythm.

Here's what the company did right: They knew what we ordered. They knew how to find out if we were happy with the order. Then they knew what questions to ask to provide the best solution for us. And they did it quickly and with the least amount of time, effort, and trouble on our part. They focused on doing the right thing for the customer.

It's in those key moments of truth—when things go wrong—where people form a relationship with your brand. Depending on how you handle those moments, the relationship can be positive or negative. This is how great business is done. Focus on the customer experience from beginning to end—Marketing, Sales, Delivery, Support, and every other touchpoint—is consistent from the customer's point of view.

If you want to know if what you're doing is working, ask yourself if it's working for the customer. Don't look at *your* success, but at your *customer's* success. According to Success Coaching, customer success is defined as "the customer's desired outcome, plus the customer's desired experience." So to satisfy customer success, the customer's desired outcome plus their desired experience has to drive all your actions. No matter how great you think your process is, if it doesn't work for the customer, it doesn't work.

> Customer success is defined as "the customer's desired outcome, plus the customer's desired experience."

Consumer business often happens this way. B2B can't imitate it perfectly and shouldn't even try. If you have a $100,000 piece of equipment that's acting up, you don't want to talk to a chatbot and drop off the part. But when you contact the company about it, you want them to be aware of the relationship they have with you. And you want their response to be driven by your desired experience and desired outcome.

WHAT'S SO DIFFERENT ABOUT B2B?

When you're shopping online in your free time or at home, it's just you and the website. The whole interaction takes place one-on-one. You log in, you search around for what you want, and you make the purchase. If it's a site you use often, they know you. They have all kinds of information about you to tailor the experience to your liking.

Buying from another business isn't that simple. You have multiple points of contact over a period of time. One day you're perusing the company's website, then you're talking to a chatbot. The next thing you know, an automatically generated email is sitting in your inbox, and you get a call from someone in Inside Sales. Soon, you're in contact with a salesperson, then Support. You could have a dozen interactions with the seller before you make a purchase. On your side of the sale, you have more interactions, like checking in with end users and decision-makers before you make a move. It's not a simple transaction like buying movie tickets on Fandango, or a bread maker on eBay, or a car on Carvana.

Every interaction is another relationship, whether it's with a person or digital. And those combined relationships form one big relationship: buyer and seller. That relationship can lead to meeting the customer's desired outcome and experience—customer success. Or it can lead to something else.

We've spent enough time talking about all the reasons "something else" happens. Let's see what *customer success* looks like.

FLOW OF INFORMATION

In a great customer experience, all of the company's systems talk to each other. When a person or a system interacts with a customer, they have visibility into the history of the relationship. If a customer calls tech support, the person who answers the phone knows whether that customer had a negative experience with the company. If a salesperson calls a customer to talk about renewals, upgrades, or upsells, they're aware of any unresolved support tickets that the customer has open with Support. With proper data flow, every point of contact is aware of all past interactions. This gives the business a chance to tailor the conversation so they don't just irritate the customer further.

The seller can even chat with Support ahead of time to see if there's an update to share. Compare "Hey, I have something to sell you," with "I know you have tickets open with us and are trying to sort things out with Support. How is that going?" or, even better, "I have good news for you! We found a workaround for that bug, and Hank's going to be getting it out to you later today." Simply acknowledging that you are aware of a problem is a million times better than pretending it doesn't exist. *Then* you can talk about the new product, or the upgrade, or that renewal.

Ideally, a salesperson who's working on renewal agreements logs in to the CRM and gets a report of customers whose renewals expire within the quarter, so they know who to contact. A summary shows how long the company has been a customer, which products are up for renewal, and the latest issues they've reported. There might be a satisfaction score, too. The salesperson clicks on the issues link to get all the details on support tickets and resolutions, and on the score to see how that number was tallied. Were there product issues? Support issues? Billing issues? Armed with this information, the salesperson can tailor the call to fit the current relationship the company has with them, and their likely mood. This is possible with data flow and a system for aggregating information from multiple points of contact in the organization, summarized to provide knowledge that's most relevant to Sales in the CRM and readily available to the salesperson when they need it.

TIMELINESS AND ACCURACY OF DATA

Having accurate information available to people who need it leads to better conversations with customers. Done right, data flow ensures that a salesperson has immediate access to information such as a customer opening a ticket, even if that ticket was opened minutes before. The details of the issue and Support's actions on it so far are at the salesperson's fingertips. Instead of being caught off guard, Sales has a complete and clear view of the customer's experience to date.

Timely, accurate data flowing across departments doesn't only assist Sales; that information can be plugged into other CX systems. For example, a chatbot that taps into the data flow pulls information to use in online conversations. Then, when a customer logs in to a company's support page, the chatbot can personalize the communication: "Hi Mr. Daniels, how can I help you today? Are you checking in on the status of support ticket #OX895 regarding the product we recently installed at your site?" As the conversation progresses, new information is added to the data flow and directed to the appropriate systems, where it can be added to reports. Think about how the customer feels after that interaction. Instead of frustrated, they're assured that the business knows them, is aware of their issues, and now has new information and will handle it. On the seller's side, speedy and accurate data integration is key to getting the right information to the right systems and making it immediately available to the people who need to see it.

CLEAR RELATIONSHIP OWNERSHIP

A customer may have one main point of contact. This person, typically a salesperson, account manager, account executive, or someone from the Support team, is responsible for the client relationship as a whole. They "own" the overall relationship and are ultimately responsible for the customer's experience, regardless of who or what else is involved in the interactions.

However, the customer shouldn't have to call that person for everything and then wait for the communication to be passed on to whoever can answer their question or solve their problem. They should know that there is a team of people to support them and have access to those people. There should be someone to answer technical questions, and someone to discuss strategy, and someone to call about billing. Again, B2B is not B2C—it's much more complex and requires more than one point of contact for the client. Identify those people. With an outside-in approach, think about why the client contacts your business, then make it clear to your people, and to the client, who owns each relationship.

Anyone the client interacts with is responsible for the relationship, but again, *one person has to own the overall relationship and be responsible for monitoring the health of that relationship.* Without this accountability, clients "fall through the cracks." Problems arise and fester, and people who can fix them might categorize them as low priority. Unresolved issues lead to an unsatisfied customer and open the door for the competition. Consistent monitoring and regular check-ins avoid a catastrophe—like losing a customer that everyone was talking to but no one was *really* listening to. The client should know who their main point of contact is. They need to have someone to call who they can count on to get things done.

Many organizations have a Client Success Team and call it a day. Or they assign someone a customer and expect that person to assume responsibility for the relationship. Responsibility is useless without knowledge authority. Before you assign ownership of a customer, consider their needs. A customer who's likely to call on technical support most often might benefit more from a main contact in Support; one who relies on your company for strategy might be happier with a point of contact with expertise and authority in that function. Again, see it from the customer's point of view and choose the person who's best equipped to deliver the outcome and experience the customer expects.

ADOPT OUTSIDE-IN THINKING

Inside-out thinking refers to putting the company's structure and functions first and expecting the customer to adjust. Outside-in thinking takes the customer's point of view and positions the business to fit their needs instead. Anyone who interacts with customers should be aware of this concept, including Marketing, Sales, Support, and Success.

Adopting this approach means subtle changes that have a dramatic effect on how the business is perceived. A warm transfer to another department, for example, including knowledge transfer to the new contact, is much better than a cold one or—worse—giving the customer a phone number and telling them to call it themselves.

Thinking outside-in goes beyond the sale and should be incorporated in any interaction. If a customer wants to return an item, don't ask them to fill out a form—give them several easy and convenient methods. Some people may prefer to make a phone call, while others will want to tap a few options on a phone app.

INSIDE-OUT THINKING CREATES HEADACHES FOR THE CUSTOMER

We recently had a frustrating experience with a health insurance provider. Even though we had purchased medical, dental, and vision insurance from a single provider, the person we spoke with at the company couldn't answer any of our dental questions because the policy was "on a different card." In a perfect world, the customer would have a single login to the company's customer portal. They would be able to make one phone call to discuss all their insurance needs, even if that meant being transferred to specialists in three different departments who had the right information on hand. There would be one billing site instead of three, and if there were one cardless service, all cards should be made available in digital form. The processes might be complicated behind the scenes, but the interface to the customer should be unified.

Another side of outside-in thinking involves company culture. Employees need the ability and authority to do what's necessary to create a positive customer experience. A system that requires people to follow a rigid set of rules that inconvenience the customer doesn't make sense. Allow people to be flexible in their solutions, so they can do what's right for the individual customer.

BRING CUSTOMERS AS CLOSE AS POSSIBLE TO THE ORGANIZATION'S DECISION-MAKING

Henry Ford said, "If I had asked people what they wanted, they would have said faster horses." Maybe...? *No*. We're not buying it.

Faster horses may have been their first answer, but if he followed up with more questions to figure out *why* they wanted faster horses, he might have discovered what they really wanted.

Outside-in thinking—starting with the customer—extends to decision-making. A company's well-intentioned decisions may affect customers in unexpected ways; inviting customers into the process can avoid negative impacts you didn't see coming.

Focus groups are underused, and though they may seem unnecessary and a drain on people's time, they are an extremely valuable method for getting your customer's input on what they care about and couldn't care less about. You might be planning to change a product's feature that your client values. Without talking to them, you won't know that.

This process looks different for every company. In some cases, customers visit with engineering or product development to share their experience with a product. Other businesses have a customer advisory board, and others use surveys. A larger business may use a combination of an advisory board, focus groups, and surveys to get a broad view of your entire customer base and more in-depth input from your major clients. However you decide to include clients in your decision-making, doing so will improve the customer experience. Remember, the definition of customer success is the customer's desired outcome plus their desired experience. Actively discussing and collecting knowledge around their desired outcomes informs your decisions around products and services.

Too often, products are launched with bells and whistles the customer doesn't care about. No matter how cool the feature is, unless it matters to the customer, it doesn't matter. If it works for the customer, it works. This doesn't mean following customers' exact orders for product development, but you have to seek their input and consider it carefully. Listening to your customers sparks innovation. It will make you conscious of problems you never knew they had that you may be able to address with a product or service. That could take your offerings in a new direction you didn't even consider.

You don't get there with a single question: *what do you want?* Ask why they want what they want and pay attention to everything they say. If Ford asked people *why* they wanted faster horses, he would have concluded that they really wanted a car. The conversation might have gone like this:

"Why do you want a faster horse? What would that horse look like, and how would it behave? Tell me about this horse that you want me to make for you."

"Well, it's faster than all the other horses. I don't have to feed it hay, and it doesn't get sick or die if I ride it too hard or too long."

"Ah, so like a machine?"

"Yeah, exactly like that."

IMAGINE WHAT'S POSSIBLE

Creating a business that works for the customer takes change. Companies have to change what they're doing now. These aren't just ideas that you carry around in your head—you have to make a plan and commit to making them happen. Stagnant, inflexible companies are going to find it hard to compete against those that embrace these changes because customers have choices, and they do not have to choose you. Even if they've been choosing you for ten years, if the competition works better for them, they will leave. For now, imagine a future where you are tuned in to your customers and discovering what they really want from you, and delivering. That's the future you get with a Revenue Takeover. Let's get into what that future looks like for your business, starting with the technology.

THE SECRET TO FOCUS GROUPS

Companies shy away from focus groups. If they saw the value, they would do them regularly. To get value from a focus group, you have to do it right. The key is to listen to every single thing customers say. Resist the urge to interpret their comments in real time and don't make any assumptions.

If a customer mentions that they wish your product did something, you cannot assume, "I think what they really mean is..." Ask more questions. Get to the root of how they really feel about your business, products, and services. Be curious enough to find out what they are really trying to tell you. The customer may not even be aware that they have more to say, so you have to keep digging.

If you ask a customer, "What would make you a customer for life?" they might say, "Never getting a bill." You can't not charge customers, of course, so ask questions around that comment. You will get to something more reasonable, such as, "I want to be able to trust you to do good work every time. I want your products to do what you promise they do, and when they don't, I want you to fix it. I only want to pay for that from you, and I want to know that you will honor the relationship we have by treating us right."

By the way, a customer who's had only good experiences with you wouldn't say this. There have obviously been problems, so probe further. What was the problem, how was it resolved, and what would they like you to have done differently? What can you do now, and what will you do going forward to ensure the problem doesn't happen again? You don't have to make these decisions in the meeting with the focus group, but let the customer know that you hear them. Then take everything from the meeting and think about it. Discuss it with your team and decide what you will do with the information.

CHAPTER 7

LINE UP BEHIND THE TECH: REVOPS

The world as we have created it is a process of our thinking. It cannot be changed without changing our thinking.

—ALBERT EINSTEIN

When Brandi's great-grandmother passed away, her great-grandmother's banker attended the funeral. He didn't just show up to pay his respects—the man sat right behind the family. This is how banking—and business in general—was done not so long ago. Touchpoints between companies and customers were very human and often one-on-one. People knew their bankers, their insurance agents, their brokers, their lawyers, and all the other people who represented the businesses they relied on. Bankers knew their clients' life stories and their families. They knew about every major life event, whether the customer was buying a house, starting a family, or planning for retirement.

These days, that personal relationship doesn't exist. Banks don't encourage people to visit their branches. Some have a limit on how many times you can use their in-person services and how many of their deposit slips you can use before they charge you a fee. People interact with banks online and with phone apps. If you do go into a bank, you will usually meet with a teller. The bankers are still there, and you can sit down with one, but they may require an appointment. Bankers work behind the scenes and are less involved with customers. The trend away from unnecessary personal interaction has further increased due to the 2020 pandemic and the associated and ongoing health, safety, and security concerns.

Today when a person dies, banks don't notice right away. Money is deposited and withdrawn automatically and electronically, so until they're notified by a relative or the authorities, a banker has no way of knowing their client has passed on.

Businesses used to be organized and lined up behind the people. Today, customer touchpoints are owned and driven by technology. Unless you need a cashier's check or a notary, you may never have to walk into a bank again.

How people manage their money has changed, and businesses that handle the money made the change possible. They put the technology in place and got behind it. Company technology is like the banker of old, who knows everything about the customer, but this only works well if the tech is centralized and centrally managed. Otherwise, customer information is spread out among many departments. A holistic strategy and system for managing the knowledge makes delivering a consistent customer experience possible, leading to more revenue.

REVENUE TECHNOLOGY AND OPERATIONS

Today's businesses have marketing technology, sales technology, and customer service technology. They purchase and manage the tech on a piecemeal basis, with teams like "Marketing Ops" and "Sales Ops" operating from within their individual departments. Managing these technologies individually creates a disjointed customer experience.

Moving away from department-owned technology to a model where any technology that supports customer interactions is centralized is what we call Revenue Technology, or *RevTech*. Imagine bringing the right people together *as a team* whose primary goal is to utilize revenue technology to enhance the experience for everyone, from a prospect in the presale stage to a loyal customer. Revenue Operations, or *RevOps*, is that team. The RevOps team sees RevTech holistically and from end-to-end to deliver a consistent, optimized customer experience and drive revenue. And to be clear, the RevOps you may be familiar with is not likely what we are talking about here. Our definition of RevOps has subtle but important differences.

REVTECH AND REVOPS

RevTech and *RevOps* are key to a Revenue Takeover. They enable companies to effectively drive revenue through customer experience.

RevTech: Revenue Technologies. These are technologies that have historically existed within departments such as Marketing, Sales, Support, Success, and other departments that directly impact the customer experience. RevTech centralizes these technologies for a holistic, end-to-end, fully enhanced customer experience that maximizes customer success and drives revenue.

RevOps: Revenue Operations. This team comprises people formerly responsible for technologies within Marketing, Sales, Support, Success, and other departments that directly impact the customer experience. Created by the centralization, organization, and management of people and processes that support RevTech at strategic, operational, and tactical levels.

REVOPS AND IT

To succeed, RevOps has to be its own department. It cannot operate as an extension of the CX teams, nor is it part of the traditional IT department, though the two must work together to share certain resources and data.

RevOps and IT have different skillsets. Both are technical, but RevOps is also well versed in Sales or Marketing, and they have a deeper connection to the needs of those departments. They also have different mandates driven by the needs of different customers. IT's customer is the organization and the people who support it, not the external customer base. In contrast, RevOps' work is driven by the external customer base and the CX teams that support it. IT's job is to provide service to the organization's technology needs. RevOps' main goal is optimizing the customer experience to drive revenue, and that team sees Marketing, Sales, Support, and Success as its internal customers.

IT projects are often large-scale, affecting the entire organization, and require a lot of planning and preparation before IT can execute. This slow, methodical approach makes sense for a department that supports company-wide networks, hardware, and software. RevOps, because they support CX teams, have to be agile and able to initiate change quickly.

REVOPS' RESPONSIBILITIES

This centralized team oversees all of the technology responsible for customer interactions, which enables revenue generation. RevOps makes sure the technologies under their control work together to support the desired customer experience. They have to be agile and respond to the needs of the CX departments and the shifts within the business environment. They are the overall governing body, with oversight of all the projects and activities on that side of the business. People and technology silos are dismantled with the creation of RevOps, and that team has to ensure they don't redevelop.

DATA, COMPLIANCE, CYBERSECURITY, AND GOVERNANCE

While both IT and RevOps are responsible for data, compliance, cybersecurity, and governance, separating ownership of these responsibilities between the front office and back office makes the design, implementation, and enforcement of protocols easier for both teams.

Laws and regulations around data, specifically *customer* data, have changed. General Data Protection Regulation (GDPR) is the most prominent example. If a customer wants to take their data back and give it to a competitor, that is their right. Fulfilling that legal requirement becomes simpler when just one team captures and maintains that data. RevOps, as stewards of RevTech, become the stewards of customer data too. The team follows the organization's broader data security rules handed down by the data privacy team and adds rules to comply with how customer data is collected, used, and protected.

This doesn't mean there are two discrete data silos. Some

data will be owned by both IT and RevOps. Transactions managed by the RevOps technology create data that a company's enterprise resource planning (ERP) system needs, and at that point, it is owned by IT. So there is overlap in data ownership. If one team suffers a data breach, it may impact the other teams, but the odds are reduced because of different layers of security protocols.

A TEAM AND TECHNOLOGY THAT ACCOMPLISH BUSINESS OBJECTIVES

Every interaction a business has with its prospects and customers is tied to a function and a department. Customer acquisition, demand generation, lead generation, sales, tech support, and other functions might be functions of Marketing, Sales, Support, and Success, or other departments. Customers cycle through many touchpoints on their way to becoming customers. A good RevOps team consistently researches technologies involved in these touchpoints even when they're not in the market for them. They evaluate the current and future needs of the business and make sure they have the right stack in place to integrate the tech, make sure the data is clean, and ensure data flow so that the right data gets to the people and systems that need it.

RevOps ensures the teams using the technology understand its purpose. This may require documentation of processes, training, and even internal certifications that prove the internal customers—the CX teams—know how to use the technology the way RevOps has designed it to be used.

Revenue Operations puts the right technology in place and lines up behind it. This, in turn, affects the organization as a whole, especially the customer experience teams. Until now, we've been referring to these individual business units as the CX teams, but really, they—*along with RevOps*—are the people that make up your front office. Let's take a look at this newly organized function—what we call the *Modern Front Office*.

CHAPTER 8

THE MODERN FRONT OFFICE

Persistent, consistent, and frequent stories, delivered to an aligned audience, will earn attention, trust, and action.

—SETH GODIN

Imagine going to market with a product your existing customers will love—one that also has the potential to draw *new* people to your door. You know how important that first impression of the product is to your customers and how important that initial interaction is to prospects. To capture as much business as possible, you work with your RevOps team to craft the perfect product launch.

To kick it off, a chatbot greets customers who log in to your site. "Hi John," it says, "How was your last support call?

Everything working fine now? Good, good. That's terrific! So happy we could help. You know, your current product expires in about a year. We're launching something new that you're going to want to see. If you have a moment, I'd love to tell you about it."

New people logging in to the site get a different message tailored to the information you have on hand around their industry, business, and role. You have ten concurrent test messages lined up, and you track the results to see which ones resonate most.

The launch draws upon data from different systems that work together to present the right message for each individual. The messaging is automated, accurate, and up-to-date because all your customer-facing technologies are integrated (RevTech) and managed by one team (RevOps). That shift in how technology is organized and managed facilitated the next step in your Revenue Takeover: the functions of Marketing, Sales, Success, and Support have been identified and intelligently integrated to form a new model for optimizing the customer experience—the Modern Front Office.

TECH INTEGRATION INFORMS ORGANIZATIONAL INTEGRATION

RevTech and RevOps centralize CX technology. Yet, the

internal end users of those technologies exist within several departments that operate under separate leadership. Coming from different directions, each department tries to connect at the focal point: the customer. The image "Front Office Today" illustrates a typical organization with four individual departments that interact with customers: *Sales, Marketing, Customer Success,* and *Customer Support.* Each department has its own technology and people to support that technology.

FRONT OFFICE TODAY

Today's typical front office reflects an analog world, with each department sitting at their own individual table, setting their own goals, and communicating the work they've accomplished to other departments "after the fact."

In contrast, the Modern Front Office begins with the customer. Its main focus is creating a positive, personalized experience by consistently communicating with prospects and customers to enhance customer success by meeting customers' and prospects' desired expectations and outcomes.

The Modern Front Office brings together the people who impact the customer experience under a single umbrella with a shared goal. It starts where product development ends, and every customer-facing department, team, and individual has a role in it beyond their departmental, team, and individual goals. They all contribute to the customer experience and, in turn, revenue.

FRONT OFFICE TOMORROW

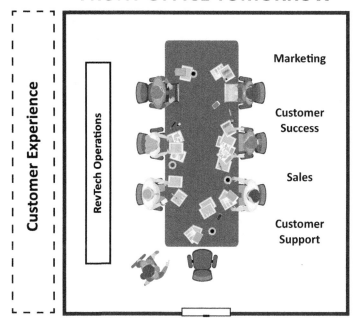

The front office of tomorrow reflects a modern, digital world where everyone is sitting at the same table, aligning their goals in real time before the work begins.

In both the traditional and the Modern Front Office, prospects and customers interact with frontline people and technology. However, in the traditional front office, different data flows to different individual departments, *and the data flow often stops there.* In the Modern Front Office, RevOps manages the revenue technology, ensuring data flow between functions.

The major shift from traditional to modern happens within the departments themselves. As illustrated in the image

"Front Office Tomorrow," Marketing, Sales, Support, and Success are still defined and exist as separate entities, *but they also have a shared goal of optimizing the customer experience to generate revenue.* They are part of one larger team with a shared priority and a more impactful company goal. Imagine how that changes the culture between the functions. All for one—the customer experience and driving revenue—and one for all.

The Modern Front Office leverages the power of RevOps and RevTech for maximum customer success. It unifies the functions of the CX teams under a single *revenue team.* Creating a revenue team allows RevOps to provide holistic customer experience-focused solutions and support to the entire team instead of spreading out its resources on an individualized basis. RevOps recognizes the individual needs of each department and function, but it also sees them as one team, and it strategizes the best approach for applying RevTech to maximize revenue.

Up till now, we've been referring to Marketing, Sales, Support, and Success as the *CX teams.* You won't hear that from us again. These are the people who make up your Modern Front Office. They—along with RevOps—are your *Revenue Team.* Capital R, capital T. Revenue Team.

In the Modern Front Office, functions that impact the customer experience, such as Marketing, Sales, Support, and Success, still exist as separate functions, but they also have a shared goal of optimizing the customer experience to generate revenue. They are your Revenue Team.

THE MODERN FRONT OFFICE VS. THE BACK OFFICE

The Modern Front Office is separate from the back office, and its management of people and technology remains separate. The back office, comprising operations, human resources, finance, legal, and all the other business functions that make a company functional, still receives its technical solutions and support from the organization's IT department. As we discussed in the previous chapter, IT owns the corporate technology infrastructure and functions that make it possible. IT makes sure everyone has a laptop, the network's up, and all the backend systems are running smoothly.

There is some overlap of data ownership between RevOps and IT, but that's just part of their relationship. In the future, RevOps and IT teams will work closely together but also not be in each other's way, as their mandates are very different. The front office is focused on the external customer and revenue generation; the RevOps team understands and supports that goal. Likewise, IT focuses on supporting the back office and ensures the smooth operation of the organization. In a traditional organizational structure, IT is being pulled in two different directions, and that results in delays and constant reprioritization of requests that come from Marketing and other revenue-impacting teams. This is one of the reasons shadow IT organizations pop up within the front office functions. RevOps solves this by being the "IT" of the Modern Front Office.

FUTURE ORGANIZATION

In the future organization, RevOps is the "IT" of the Modern Front Office.

GAME CHANGER

Saying your business is focused on the customer experience isn't enough. Running a new technology or initiative to make the customer happy won't cut it. You literally have to change the organization. Starting with the technology, RevOps, and the creation of the Modern Front Office, staying in the game requires changing how you interact externally, and more importantly, how you operate internally. This is a huge game changer.

CHAPTER 9

THE DOMINO EFFECT

For the want of a nail the shoe was lost,
For the want of a shoe the horse was lost,
For the want of a horse the rider was lost,
For the want of a rider the battle was lost,
For the want of a battle the kingdom was lost,
And all for the want of a horseshoe-nail.

—BENJAMIN FRANKLIN

Have you ever lined up a set of dominos? You know, where you set up the tiles to create a certain formation? If you do it right, you can knock the first domino down and it impacts the second one, knocking it down. That domino impacts the third one and so on until all the dominos are down. The result is a twisting, turning line of dominos, each one an individual tile, yet connected by design.

That doesn't happen by accident. You have to align each consecutive domino with the one before it. Spacing is important too: the tiles must be close enough together so each one impacts the next, but far enough apart to allow them room to fall. The domino effect doesn't require a massive effort. Placed correctly, a gentle nudge is all it takes to create the formation. Then, working together in perfect alignment, each domino contributes to the final results. The formation is greater than each individual tile, yet it is not possible if just one is removed.

In the Modern Front Office model of a Revenue Takeover, a business operates like a set of dominos. All the functions within the customer life cycle—from lead, to sales, to customer experience—line up closely enough to impact one another yet far enough apart to move freely. Together, they create a perfect formation: your Revenue Team. A Revenue Team can be small, a dozen people or so from all your former CX teams, or comprise thousands across global sites. Positioned correctly, each individual and function impacts the next, creating a perfect design. The many functions of a Revenue Team work closely together to benefit from the momentum.

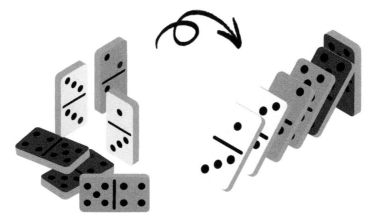

In the Modern Front Office model of a Revenue Takeover, a business operates like a set of dominos with all the functions within the customer life cycle—from lead, to sales, to customer experience—lined up.

THE DOMINO EFFECT AND THE REVENUE TEAM

Like dominos, Revenue Team players must communicate with the players ahead of them and behind them. One person or function's output feeds into the next, so each must be aware of where they fit in the lineup. Each must also see the "grand design" and how they fit in that as well. Aligned functions—like aligned dominos—work together to create the desired end result.

Enough about dominos. Let's look at a real-world example of the process in action. A typical inbound marketing strategy might have four functions: *Attract*, *Convert*, *Close*, and *Delight*. Within those functions are subfunctions. Your inbound strategy may have different functions and subfunctions, but the overall goal is likely similar: turning prospects into customers and, ultimately, enthusiastic brand ambassadors. For that to happen, each function (for example, *Convert*) must align with the function that feeds it (*Attract*), as well as the function it feeds (*Close*). The people comprising these functions must also understand their place in the grand design.

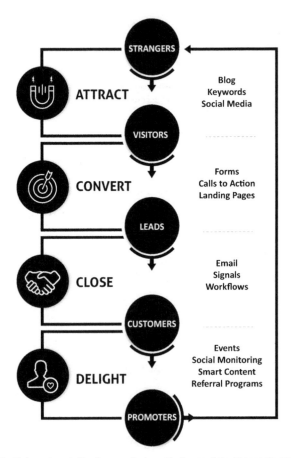

A standard inbound marketing framework shows the journey from stranger to promoter.

ATTRACT

The goal of the *Attract* function is to turn strangers into visitors. The subfunctions, people, and technology in this stage of inbound marketing strategy attract net new people to the business. They do this by engaging more eyes and more interest to make people aware of the brand, what it stands for, and what the company has to offer. They encourage new people to visit the business's content via the website, marketing collateral, campaigns, and in person.

KEY ATTRACT SUBFUNCTIONS

Key subfunctions within this stage are social media, public relations, and the company website. A business may have a corporate marketing or brand team, people to manage the website, and people to manage events. In smaller companies, teams may manage several subfunctions.

ATTRACT MEASURES

Net new contacts in the database is a vital metric. The *Attract* stage strives to entice a certain number of new visitors to the brand and new names into the pipeline: people with whom the company can begin purposeful conversations. In addition, *Attract* measures consider the following online engagement metrics:

- How people engage on social media

- How people engage with the website
- What people click on and view
- Where visitors to social media channels and the website come from geographically, and their demographics
- How long people spend on the site, whether they return after an initial visit, and how often they return
- How "deep" they go into a site: are they viewing only the main page or clicking deeper and bingeing content? The deeper a person goes in a session and the more often they return, the more impactful it is to the business.

This is not just about tracking the numbers, because having a lot of names in your database means nothing if those people aren't your target market or aren't interested in what you have to offer because you are not providing them with engaging content. Contacts that count are relevant and engaged. Quality matters more than quantity.

Looking ahead to the next stage, *Convert*: if you can't convert the people you're pulling into the database with the *Attract* function, you will not deliver what the next stage needs to do its job. Like a domino that doesn't fall, the *Attract* stage won't have an impact on the *Convert* stage, and the inbound marketing strategy won't achieve its goal.

CONVERT

In inbound marketing, *conversion* doesn't refer to converting prospects to customers, but converting people you've attracted in the *Attract* stage to leads. In the *Convert* stage, you capture and raise levels of interest ranging from clear hand raisers to people who have implied interest, based on the key metrics discovered in the earlier stage.

KEY CONVERT SUBFUNCTIONS

The *Convert* stage's subfunctions include *Demand* (or *Lead*) *Generation* and *Digital Marketing*. Worth mentioning here is that the people working on a strategy don't always sit within just one function. The web development team, for example, might have responsibilities within both the *Attract* and the *Convert* stages.

CONVERT MEASURES

Many metrics can fall under the *Convert* stage and its subfunctions. Depending on the industry and sales process, companies might track many more than the two key ones, "hand raisers" and "Marketing Qualified Leads."

- Hand raisers have explicitly stated their interest. Essentially, this is a lead.
- Marketing Qualified Leads refers to people who have implicitly expressed some interest in a company's products or service.

In the *Convert* stage, you are looking at the number and percentage of contacts captured in the *Attract* stage that you were able to qualify as, or convert to, hand raisers or Marketing Qualified Leads.

CLOSE

The *Close* stage is where you try to turn leads into customers. This is where Marketing and Sales usually cross over.

KEY CLOSE SUBFUNCTIONS

Inside Sales or Lead Development usually lives in this stage, working with Marketing and Sales departments such as Campaign Execution, Sales Support, and Sales Engineering to make sure the customer is getting the right products and services to close the deal.

CLOSE MEASURES

Close measures are not only "closed deals" or "new customers," though those are important metrics. Rather, in this stage, the team looks at the opportunities created in the *Convert* stage and where they exist in the pipeline.

- Of the hand raisers and Marketing Qualified Leads, how many new opportunities exist, and what are the percentages of each?

- Where are they in the sales funnel: demo, scoping, pricing? You might have a dozen different stages within your sales funnel. Look at each one as a domino impacting the next.
- How big were the opportunities initially, and how big are they now?
- How long did it take them to get to Sales? How long have they been with Sales?
- What percentage of the deals are closing? Of those that close, how long did it take to close?
- What does the final dollar amount look like compared to the initial forecasted value?
- What is the average timeline from initial interaction to closed deal?

Once a lead has been closed, Marketing's job isn't over. The final stage is also the most commonly neglected one, yet it can have the greatest impact on the Revenue Team's performance.

DELIGHT

This stage turns customers into promoters. Delighting customers drives retention, repeat buys, upsells, and referrals. *Delight* includes many activities, from onboarding new clients through support, plus events outside the traditional customer life cycle, such as engaging people on customer advisory boards and focus groups and inviting them to company events.

WHEN NUMBERS LIE

Rolly once worked with an organization that planned to generate $2M from a single event. The goal was to convert fifty executives, primarily CIOs and CHROs (Chief Human Resource Officers), into ten leads and to close two deals from those leads at $1M each.

This required a lot of contacts in the *Attract* stage, and the thinking was, "The more emails we have, the better." The company bought emails from a number of sources and ended up with over 5,000 names to throw over the fence to the *Convert* stage.

In this stage, the company only converted twenty-three people, so they knew their $2M goal probably wouldn't be met. But with twenty-three high-level executives in the room, they were still hopeful that the event would generate a healthy return on their investment.

The real surprise came when these people showed up at the event. You see, anyone can plug the title "CIO," "CEO," or "CHRO" into their LinkedIn profile or add it to their signature block. Many of these people *are* "executives"—basically, CEOs of a company in which they are the sole employee, and they're running the business out of their living room. That's exactly who showed up at the event. Sure, the attendees were enthusiastic about getting some freebies from the company, but none of them were prepared to spend a million bucks.

If you didn't look closely at what each stage was doing or measure the right things, you might think they killed it in the *Attract* stage and that it was the people in the *Convert* stage that dropped the ball. Or that the people in the *Convert* stage, by delivering twenty-three executives, did at least a good enough job to generate $1M from the event, in which case the *Close* stage fell apart. The fact is, of those 5,000 emails, it's likely that none were the right targets for the event.

KEY DELIGHT SUBFUNCTIONS

Anyone who plays a role in supporting current customers has a role in *Delight*, from customer success managers to support representatives to marketing account executives and more.

DELIGHT MEASURES

Companies usually have key measures around *Attract*, *Convert*, and *Close*, but few track metrics around *Delight*. Following are a few we've seen at this stage:

- Unprompted Positive Feedback, which is unprompted, organically provided, positive feedback. This is not the result of a survey or questionnaire, but an email, phone call, social media post, or review where, for example, a client reaches out to let you know how pleased they are with your business, product, or something someone on your team did for them. You might be on a call with a client who says, "Hey, we had a little glitch here last week, and Jane over in tech support solved the problem right away. We were back up and running in no time." These kinds of comments might make you smile, but you should capture them and count them.
- Attrition or Churn Rate. This is the number and percentage of customers that shrink, stagnate, or go away.
- Share of Wallet. This metric refers to how much of your available products and services your customer is

buying. They may be using just one product, yet they have a need for another one. If they're getting it from another company, there is an opportunity for you to gain a greater share of wallet.

Tracking metrics and KPIs is important, but it's not the final measure of the success of a function. To evaluate the success of *Attract*, *Convert*, *Close*, or *Delight*, look at their metrics and KPIs against the output of the previous function and that of the following function. Likewise, to measure the success of a subfunction, compare its metrics and KPIs against the output of the subfunctions preceding and following it.

The benefit of this is that it gives you a truer picture of each subfunction's impact and its KPI success. As an example, if the demand generation team—part of *Convert*—has a Marketing Qualified Leads goal of, say, a hundred new leads a month, they could easily manipulate their definition of an MQL to meet the goal. However, looking at what happens within that subfunction, if they fail to elevate any of those Marketing Qualified Leads to hand raisers, meeting the hundred MQLs goal doesn't sound so impressive. Likewise, looking ahead to the next subfunction, if they did turn half of those MQLs into hand raisers and passed them on to *Close*, yet none of them actually closed, then they have nothing to brag about. Looking at the previous subfunction, say that *Attract* had delivered *two thousand* net new contacts. In this case, *Convert* turning those contacts into just a hundred Marketing Qualified Leads is actually dismal and probably falls far short of the company's expectations.

Instead of focusing on the numbers, look at the percentage of deliverables in comparison to the deliverables that came before the subfunction, as well as in comparison to the ones that follow.

This is the domino effect. By changing how you measure success—not by the individual function, but by its success in relation to the success of its surrounding functions' outputs—you promote functions that work for the whole to create the design you need.

The level at which you track metrics and their impact is up to you. The closer you look, the more you are apt to discover. If your deals aren't big enough, you could track the issue back to the website. It could be that products are presented individually on the site, with no connection to other products or services, so the customer isn't aware that they work together or even that those other products exist.

Making those connections flushes out the issues within each function. Once you've identified them, you can do something about them. But without seeing how one domino impacts—or does not impact—another, they may never make themselves apparent.

LET THE DOMINOS FALL

Seeing your Revenue Team through the lens of the domino effect changes how goals are approached by leaders, teams, and individual contributors. Instead of seeing your goal as "isolated," you see it as part of the whole design. This, in turn, changes how you see your role in the success of functions, teams, and departments beyond your traditional sphere of influence and how you see it as a contributor to the company's revenue.

This also shifts accountability. It actually gives *visibility* to accountability. Instead of teams pointing fingers at each other for missed goals, you are tracking success down the line and where shortfalls occur becomes obvious.

Teams that are doing their jobs welcome this shift. Those struggling may not because they will have nowhere to hide. However, this can also bring to light issues with training or leadership, which you can address now that you see them.

Initiating the domino effect begins with strategy and planning, where you look at the bigger goals and track them back to the individual goals and functions. It also requires some training so that every "domino" understands the objectives of their fellow dominos and how they impact them. They also should see the big picture—the grand design you have planned when all the dominos fall together.

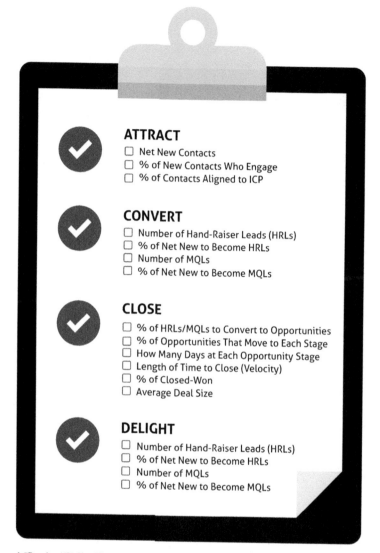

ATTRACT
- ☐ Net New Contacts
- ☐ % of New Contacts Who Engage
- ☐ % of Contacts Aligned to ICP

CONVERT
- ☐ Number of Hand-Raiser Leads (HRLs)
- ☐ % of Net New to Become HRLs
- ☐ Number of MQLs
- ☐ % of Net New to Become MQLs

CLOSE
- ☐ % of HRLs/MQLs to Convert to Opportunities
- ☐ % of Opportunities That Move to Each Stage
- ☐ How Many Days at Each Opportunity Stage
- ☐ Length of Time to Close (Velocity)
- ☐ % of Closed-Won
- ☐ Average Deal Size

DELIGHT
- ☐ Number of Hand-Raiser Leads (HRLs)
- ☐ % of Net New to Become HRLs
- ☐ Number of MQLs
- ☐ % of Net New to Become MQLs

A "Domino KPI Checklist" shows the most common KPIs at each stage of the journey and may be used as a starting point for "lining up the dominos."

CHAPTER 10

THE "OPEN CONCEPT" REVENUE TEAM

The strength of the team is each individual member. The strength of each member is the team.

—PHIL JACKSON

Do you remember how homes used to be structured? Not so many decades ago, houses had a lot of rooms with walls between them. The kitchen was a boxed-in space with a door. So were the living room, dining room, and all the bedrooms. If you had a dinner party back then, you prepared the hors d'oeuvres (you know, the apps!) in the kitchen and carried them out to your guests in the living room. Then you went back into the kitchen to finish cooking the meals—one course after another—and you carried all that into the dining room. After the meal, you might ask partygoers to move out of the dining room and back into the living room for cocktails. Dinner party hosts did a lot of running around between rooms back then. That left little time to visit with their guests.

Then came the open concept floor plan. Suddenly, all the walls were down. Guests grabbed appetizers from the kitchen and chatted with the host. They pitched in to help with the cooking and cleanup, talking and laughing together. A conversation that started in the living room was joined by a voice in the dining room and finished by someone stirring a drink in the kitchen. Everyone could see everyone else, and communication flowed freely.

This is what it's like to go from a *traditional* approach to revenue to the *Revenue Team of the future* (minus the cocktails, unless your organization promotes that sort of thing). Sounds lovely, doesn't it? It is. Getting there isn't simple, though. If you start your business from the ground up with an open concept Revenue Team, the pieces fall into place. But most companies are still structured like a 1950s farmhouse, with a lot of rooms and a lot of walls—some of them being load-bearing walls.

You can keep your old farmhouse as-is and still generate revenue. You'll have your kitchen for cooking and your dining room for eating and your living room for socializing.

It still works. It just works a lot better if you knock down those walls.

There is no shortcut here. You can have everything else we've talked about in this business of the future, but it will fall short without an open concept Revenue Team. You will have to get out the sledgehammer and get to work. Drywall will fly. Plumbing will need to be rerouted, and wiring rewired. Unlike an old farmhouse, though, you probably won't find anything too scary like mold, or a skeleton, or a trap door leading to the haunted root cellar. You'll still have all the rooms, and all the people, and all the tech, but they will be able to see and hear and talk to each other.

The major reason companies would resist the open concept Revenue Team is the status quo. Keeping things as they are is *so* attractive. Not like moving everything around, reconfiguring, and maybe putting some other priorities on hold. Leaders have never found it easy to change a structure that's been in place for years or generations because they know how hard it is and sticking with what works well enough is so much easier.

This is an all-or-nothing proposition. You can't just widen a doorway or cut a hole in the wall. It's decision time, and you can stay where you are and, well, stay where you are. Or you can accept that taking down those walls will be hard and maybe painful, but once it's accomplished, you'll have the most beautiful home on the block.

NOTHING WILL EVER FEEL THE SAME

You know what a lot of a Revenue Takeover looks like, from outside-in strategies to centralized ownership of revenue technologies (RevTech), to the Modern Front Office and the Domino Effect. You can have that future, but creating an open concept Revenue Team is how *major change* happens. Once you do it, nothing will ever feel the same. The visibility opens up, and you have access to information, people, and functions that you didn't know about or didn't know were important to you and how the company generates revenue. You will have the big picture of how everything works. With no barriers, the flow of information surges along with the feeling that everyone is "in it" together for the benefit of each other and the business. Suddenly, everyone *gets it*.

We can't emphasize enough the shift in attitudes that happens when you bring all your customer experience people under the Revenue Team umbrella. When a salesperson asks Marketing for better collateral, Marketing won't roll their eyes; they will have a clear picture of how supporting Sales impacts their own KPIs. When a marketing person asks Sales for more information on their customers, Sales won't say they're too busy because they will understand how taking time to help Marketing affects their success.

And everyone will see the connection between their actions, customer success, and revenue.

When people know that other people have a vested interest in helping them, they're more likely to ask for help, too. A Success person, for example, won't hesitate to pick up the phone to check in with a Support person on a customer's ticket status. Simply knowing that everyone on the Revenue Team has everyone else's back creates a more cohesive, positive, and action-oriented culture. The barriers are down. The "us against them" attitude goes out the window. Everyone is on the same team—the happy customers and more revenue team.

There is new transparency, too, which brings with it vulnerability. The open concept Revenue Team exposes weaknesses in teams. It shows you where people need more training and resources and where you may not have the right people with the right skills in all the right jobs. Expect that to happen, and be prepared to manage it head-on, not as a weakness, but as an opportunity for vast improvements.

LOOK UPSTREAM TO SOLVE DOWNSTREAM PROBLEMS

With the open concept Revenue Team in place, tackling revenue problems isn't limited to where they appear. Say you're in Sales, and your deal sizes aren't growing at the pace you need to meet a *Close* stage KPI. A salesperson on a traditional sales team might look at current deals to identify opportunities to add more products, services, and service contracts. That tactical approach is limited, and even if it's successful, it solves only one problem for one customer and one deal at a time.

As part of the Revenue Team, the salesperson has other functions to look to for assistance. They can go to the marketing teams and say, "This is the problem I'm having, and I need your help. What can we do at an earlier stage in the process to grow my deal sizes?" Because everyone is part of the Revenue Team, they will be open to hearing this request and motivated to help solve it. Bigger deals reflect well on their KPIs too. And if they can make an adjustment that solves a problem for one client, they can probably solve that same problem for many clients, effecting a more dramatic positive impact on revenue.

EVERYONE BECOMES YOUR ACCOUNTABILITY PARTNER

The open concept structure of the Revenue Team promotes a collaborative mindset. Instead of pointing fingers, people look inward for how they can better support the team. Instead of seeing other departments as outsiders, team members see them as insiders that can help a person get the job done better.

THE LADY FOOT LOCKER MODEL

When Brandi managed a Lady Foot Locker years ago, she taught her sales associates to always sell the socks with the shoes. The socks appeared with the shoes in the advertising. They were prominently placed near the cash register so customers couldn't miss them. And the salespeople grabbed them off the rack to verify the customer wanted to add them to their purchase. Most people said "yes." Who doesn't want a fresh new pair of socks to go with their brand new shoes? Especially after seeing them in commercials, on posters, and right there at the register?

Many marketing and sales techniques work in any industry—from shoe sales to car sales to high tech sales. They work even better when they work together. When Marketing, Sales, Support, and Success all work together, everybody puts more money in the cash register.

Have you tried to accomplish something really hard? Like losing weight, starting a new exercise regimen, or training for a big race? Doing something this difficult can be easier with an accountability partner who's as invested in your success as you are. Even though they have nothing to personally gain by your achievement, they agree to hold you accountable to that diet, that gym habit, or that daily run.

This is what it's like on a Revenue Team. People hold one another accountable for doing their best. By the same token, people are inspired to do their best because they don't want to let the team down. The cool thing is how naturally this happens. It's not like having a boss over your head demanding you do your part or a coworker sneering at you because you're doing too much.

The accountability crosses departmental lines, too. Instead of lobbing leads over the proverbial fence and hoping Sales does something with them, Marketing first talks to Sales about what they want in a lead. They might change what they're doing to get better leads, and after they pass them to Sales, they check in to see whether they got what they needed. Likewise, if Sales is going to an event, they talk to Marketing about the event ahead of time. What are they promoting? What are Marketing's goals with the event, how do they expect to achieve them, and what can Sales do to help?

The line of sight on the Revenue Team personalizes the work. You're not just passing your leads to Sales—you're passing them to Tim, Elijah, and Jennifer. They are counting on you for good leads, and you are counting on them to follow up. Yes, your KPIs and professional success depend on it, but as a human being, you also just want to see these other people succeed.

Remember the old traditional home with all the walls? Say there's another dinner party. Peter and Ollie invited all their friends to the party, and afterward they're going to the lounge. The hosts do all the cooking and the serving. They make the after-dinner cocktails, pass them around, then head back into the dining room to clear the dishes. Meanwhile, everyone's waiting to go to the lounge, but they can't leave without the hosts. The next stop for Peter and Ollie is the kitchen, where they have to put away all the leftovers and load the dishwasher. It's getting late, and the guests are getting antsy. What's taking Peter and Ollie so long?

Next door, in the open concept house, there's another party going on. Since there are no barriers in that home, the guests can see Sammy and Keisha cleaning up, and everyone pitches in to help. They make it to the lounge and get right in. An hour later, Peter and Ollie's friends show up and have to wait in line. They're a little tipsy because they drank too much waiting for the hosts, and half of them step out of line and take a Lyft home.

Do you think anyone at Sammy and Keisha's complained about having to help with the dishes? Or do you think they were happy to pitch in so everyone could get to the lounge? Whose dinner party was the greatest success? Which house does everyone want to go to next weekend?

This is a culture-changing move. Work isn't a dinner party, drinks, and the lounge, but it can be a lot more enjoyable—and people can be more accountable—when everyone sees the impact their actions have on one another.

CELEBRATING THE WINS AND THE LOSSES

In our previous careers, working for other businesses, we had a lot of big marketing wins. One that stands out for Brandi is a quarter when her team blew their lead count and conversions out of the water. They usually did well, but this time was particularly memorable because, in the same quarter, Sales missed the business revenue goal by a significant amount. So while Brandi's people were eating cake and ice cream and chatting about how they were going to spend their bonuses, Sales was in the next room, wondering whether they would still have jobs by the end of the day. Brandi's team enjoyed the cake, but they would have enjoyed it a lot more if they could have shared it with Sales.

Creating a Revenue Team doesn't ensure that every department will hit its goals or miss them completely, but it shifts ownership of the wins and losses to everyone. A win by Marketing is due in part to actions by Sales and vice versa. Likewise, a missed revenue goal is everyone's responsibility, no matter who fell short on their metrics. And while this shift in ownership will happen organically, it is the leaders among the Revenue Team who set the tone and send the signal, "Each and every one of us has a hand in the success and failure of our colleagues. We share the successes and the failures. This is how we behave and how we treat one another on the Revenue Team."

NOT EVERYONE THRIVES IN THIS ENVIRONMENT

Some people struggle in this collaborative environment. There are employees who are happy to focus on their corner of the business and don't feel comfortable thinking about anything else or taking responsibility for work beyond their defined tasks. That is all they know and all they want to do. They may shine in their current position, but only because no one has ever measured them in relation to the "dominos" they impact.

Low performers may also struggle, but only if they don't want to do more. People who see the opportunity to capitalize on the support of the team and grow into their role can do very well. But those who are not productive and have been able to "hide" in a partitioned structure may suddenly find themselves outed.

The open concept Revenue Team requires a different way of thinking, working, and communicating. People who prefer their "walls" for whatever reason will not thrive.

SHIFT TIME AWAY FROM TASKS THAT DO NOT CONTRIBUTE TO REVENUE

When the goal of all these people, teams, and departments is "revenue," that is what everyone thinks about and weighs their decisions against. It's how they spend their time and resources because it's front-of-mind *every single day*. Tasks that don't contribute to revenue—or to the customer experience, driving revenue—are exposed as less important or meaningless, and people either spend less time on them or stop doing them completely. When everybody has the same priority, there is no debate around what's important.

THIS IS EMOTIONAL

Renovations are messy. Tearing down walls is hard. None of this is *necessary*. You can leave the walls up or just upgrade the kitchen. Make one really good department—Marketing, Sales, Support. The people in that department will flourish, and if that's the only department and the only people your leaders care about, they might be okay with that. Great leaders aren't like that. They see the possibilities of the whole business and want to reach higher and wider.

Expect emotions to run high. Expect people to doubt you. Expect some people to quit. Whoever initiates the Revenue Takeover and takes on the creation of the Revenue Team may not be the most popular person at work for a while. That person has to see it and understand why it works and why they have to do it. They see how the Revenue Team is a game changer and worth all the blood, sweat, and tears it takes to make it happen.

Yes, it's hard. But there are steps that make it less hard. They're laid out in the rest of this book, so you don't have to figure it out on your own. We'll show you the four phases to getting from where you are now to where you can be, with a Revenue Takeover that breaks down all the barriers that limit your people and your revenue.

There is one person who can make it happen—the person reading this book. Are you ready to knock down the walls? Grab your sledgehammer.

PART III

HOW YOU GET THERE

By now, you see what's possible for the future of B2B Marketing. You know how it will affect customer experience and revenue. Going from the traditional revenue structure to a strategy that accounts for all the people, functions, and technology of every revenue stream to create a collaborative, synergistic, revenue-driving powerhouse is a process. Pick your path, then follow the phased approach laid out in this section to go from revenue supporter team to Revenue Takeover hero—and from CMO to CRO.

CHAPTER 11

PICK YOUR PATH

No matter how long you've been going down the wrong path, turn around.

—TURKISH PROVERB

There is no definitive map that shows you how to get from all the problems in Part 1 to the amazing future described in Part 2—basically, how to stage your own Revenue Takeover. Everyone's business is different. Each one's customer experience teams are different. You'll be starting this journey at one point—another CMO will start from somewhere else. But the outposts along the path are the same. If you're like most businesses we've worked with, you probably share the same problems around technology, customer experience, and revenue. That's where our expertise lies, and while we won't draw you a map, we will show you the outposts that solve these problems and how to reach them. The exact path you take will be up to you.

These outposts, or phases, follow a method we've developed working with a lot of companies to create and deliver an exceptional customer experience. As you've learned, a Modern Front Office promotes an optimized customer experience, which leads to growth. That's the path you should be on: the path to happy customers and revenue growth.

"Revenue Takeover" is a simple concept that requires wrapping your arms around all the elements of your business that touch the customer and affect revenue. However, it's a complex, four-phase, step-by-step process that requires a patient and tailored approach.

The Revenue Takeover has four phases, but there's also an overriding reality that permeates each phase: *your customers are unique*. So we want you to shift your focus away from growth and turn it outward to the customer and how they experience your business. Your objective is to grow the business, but not in the usual ways. If you take the typical path of investing in a big ad campaign, taking on investors, or buying another company, you'll still have the same problems we discussed in Part 1. In contrast, a Revenue Takeover creates a foundation for sustainable, predictable growth that considers the customer and scales.

This method doesn't rely on coming out with a product that catches on or landing a huge client. There's no luck involved. It's methodical, and it works.

An optimized customer experience leads to growth, and that's the path you should be on: *the path to happy customers and growth.*

YOUR REVENUE TAKEOVER, IN FOUR PHASES

The path to a Revenue Takeover involves four phases. These phases are flexible, so they work for any business regardless of the current situation and starting point. The phases allow for the companies' differences in leadership and business units. They also allow for different performance metrics and priorities between industries.

WE'LL SET THE FOUNDATION, YOU BRING THE SOY MILK—OR THE WORMS

To see the difference between traditional customer experience improvements and a Revenue Takeover, take a chain coffee shop, for example, where each store operates as an individual business unit, yet all are accountable to the same KPIs such as profit or items sold. On a scatter chart, the bell curve is wide and stretches from criminally bad performance on the left to lightspeed performance on the far right. This is the state of a coffee shop chain where no one has taken the time to do anything revolutionary to help elevate that broad spectrum of failure and success—*done what's necessary to bring up those poor performers.* A coffee shop that relies on the same old "improvements"—like cookie-cutter scripts so that baristas say the same words to every customer, standardized policies and procedures that are strictly adhered to with no exceptions, and identical upselling processes that every employee has to walk the customer through—don't make significant changes to that bell curve. They have to do something else—something harder, but more impactful.

Of course, many traditional rules of thumb still work very well, such as having each store laid out similarly so customers know where to find what they want, and using the same type of lighting, ambience, and so on so the customer knows they're "in your store." But to shift the bell curve to the right, with more high performers and less variability, you have to do something very counterintuitive: instead of standardizing, you have to allow for more variability in metrics. You have to capitalize on each shop's *uniqueness.*

This means lightening up on the standardization and allowing each store to cater to their particular customers. One place may have a lot of customers who are lactose intolerant or vegan. Why not allow that place to offer a non-dairy alternative, like soy milk? Another place may be located in a rural area where—oddly enough—people are always looking to buy live bait. If the store manager thinks selling fish and worms at the counter is a good idea (and you can get it approved by the health department), figure out how to make that happen. Is another store's workforce primarily an older crowd? Let the store manager refine the script, processes, and employee training to fit the team.

Ultimately, a Revenue Takeover's success depends on how you adapt it to your business, your customers, your people. We'll give you the layout and the lighting. It will be up to you to decide whether you want to sell worms.

HIGHLY PRESCRIPTIVE
MANAGEMENT AND METHODS

FLEXIBLE
MANAGEMENT AND METHODS

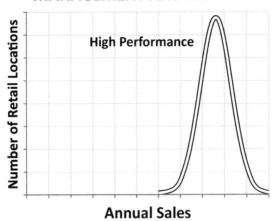

A Revenue Takeover starts from the outside—the customer—and emphasizes the uniqueness of your customer base and their expected experiences and outcomes. Customer success relies on shifting away from standardization and toward emphasizing what makes your customers different and your business special to them. This is the hard part, but it's required to move the bell curve of performance to the right.

"Revenue Takeover" is a simple concept that requires wrapping your arms around all the elements of your business that touch the customer and affect revenue. However, it's a complex, four-phase, step-by-step process that requires a patient and tailored approach.

HOW IT'S DONE

The Revenue Takeover is done with an outside-in approach, starting with the customer and working inward. This requires looking at the customers' needs and figuring out how to satisfy them with the right tech, team, organization, and leadership.

Chapter 12, "Have the Right Tech," is Phase 1 of the Revenue Takeover: By focusing on the customer experience, defining use cases to support it, then identifying the best technology to satisfy those use cases, you can deliver superior results for the customer. You might need help from a consultant or technologist for this phase, but laying a solid foundation for a Revenue Takeover is critical to its success.

Chapter 13, "Building RevOps," covers Phase 2 of the Revenue Takeover: Technology that touches the customer cannot be managed effectively on a piecemeal basis—it requires a holistic vision and team to strategize and execute for the best experience and opportunities for revenue growth. Your RevOps team may comprise members of departments like Marketing and Sales, who are now also part of the Modern Front Office, your Revenue Team.

**Chapter 14, "What REAL Change Looks Like,"
describes Phase 3:** In this phase, the barriers that currently
divide what will become the Modern Front Office—Marketing, Sales, Service, Support, and now, RevOps—come
tumbling down. Goal setting and planning are done individually for each function, but also *transparently* and
collaboratively to create alignment, avoid overlap and gaps,
capitalize on synergies, and ensure communication and
data flow. Working together to have a shared vision for
meeting corporate objectives serves as the North Star for
individual initiatives.

**Chapter 15, "Introducing the Chief Revenue Officer," is
the final phase of the Revenue Takeover:** Revenue that
depends on RevOps and the Modern Front Office needs
great leadership. The right person for this role has broad
vision, an understanding of how each function within the
Revenue Team operates, and enough technical knowledge
to lead a technical team. Without a leader accountable for
customer experience and revenue, no one will own it. This
is the hardest phase if you have issues with culture, communication, or leadership. However, success in the first
three phases smooths the path for an easier Phase 4. By this
point in the process, that person will likely have revealed
themselves from your current leadership team. This is not
a traditional CRO role. It's the CRO of the future.

A rigid methodology that claims to solve customer experience problems and boost revenue is arrogant at best—misleading and irresponsible at worst. This is why the Revenue Takeover is not a one-size-fits-all solution. Rather, it allows for variations, so the more you tailor it to fit your company, the better the results. Rely on your in-depth, insider knowledge of your company's leadership, industry, culture, and people to roll out each of the four phases in a way that capitalizes on the opportunities and compensates for the challenges.

Standardized applications of metrics do not account for differences and do not capitalize on a business's unique qualities that could lead to improved performance. A different approach—like putting soy milk and live bait on the menu—can be difficult for a company with multiple sites that is trying to standardize operations and provide a consistent customer experience, but an individual business has this opportunity.

The time for putting Band-Aids on customer issues is long past. Waiting for the planets to line up and the universe to deliver the right product or customer is wishful thinking. You may actually be on a growth path and seeing good results, but where does that path lead? Is it sustainable? Or is it a temporary route that sees you through to the next quarter?

If you're on the wrong path, you can turn around. There's another path to take, and in the next four chapters we'll show you what it looks like and how you get there. This is the Revenue Takeover that frees you from the problems of the past and moves you forward with a competitive edge that's sustainable, scalable, and built for growth.

CHAPTER 12

HAVE THE RIGHT TECH

It is no use saying, "We are doing our best." You have got to succeed in doing what is necessary.

—WINSTON CHURCHILL

Phase 1 of a Revenue Takeover is having the right tech. That starts with your technology purchases. Typically, technology purchases are based on business needs, right? You would think that's how it happens, but more often, they're not. Familiarity, adverse selection, minimum requirement RFPs, fear of missing out on the latest gadget, and compromise are the overriding decision-makers when it comes to buying new tech.

People like to buy whatever they've used before. So if your people used some software at one company, they'll want to use it at yours. Or there's a hot new technology out there that everyone's talking about. The tech vendor is sponsoring conferences, and their CEO is on the speaking circuit. FOMO takes over and whoever's in charge of tech purchases is convinced that they have to have it.

Then there's the worst-case scenario for tech decisions: a request for proposal (RFP) process driven by procurement. A survey is conducted to capture basic requirements and the purchase made without any true understanding of the actual business needs. Sometimes the decision is a foregone conclusion because the RFP is actually written by the vendor. You know it happens. Even in situations that aren't corrupt, RFP processes are notorious for adverse selection, with the worst possible vendors and tech getting through the process. In other words, vendors that discount anything and even make things up to pass a stage in the selection are the ones that get the deal. RFPs can set you up to get the worst possible technology partner and solution.

Choices are often relationship-driven too. If a decision-maker works with a vendor they like, they're going to keep buying from that person regardless of whether they have the best solution for the business needs.

People are busy, and they're tired, and they're distracted. Faced with a technology purchase, they focus on the path of least resistance. If you need to deploy emails and you have a CRM in place, you opt for the marketing automation tool add-on. If you're trying to make a decision about a solution and the only other person in the room is the vendor selling it, you will not likely make the best choice. Whether or not it's the right tech is not a priority. Instead, it's "How fast can I get it? What does it cost? How quickly can we implement it? What's the contract process?" The answers take precedence in the technology choice.

Winston Churchill had it right: "It is no use saying, 'We are doing our best.' You have got to succeed in doing what is necessary." New tech might help you get something done and make you think you're doing your best. But that isn't enough, especially when there are other choices that can help you do it so much better, faster, and smarter. That's where doing what's necessary comes in—making the harder choices that pay off with better outcomes than you've been settling for...or could even imagine.

We're not going to tell you that there's one best solution for everyone. Even a best-in-class technology may not be the best choice for your business needs. Thousands of technologies exist because there are thousands of needs, and every business has its own particular use cases to satisfy. So we won't recommend you buy this tech or that—we don't know you or what you need. We do know that if you're like every business we've worked with, you probably have some technology that was purchased the wrong way for the wrong reasons.

START WITH A TECHNOLOGY ASSESSMENT AND VALIDATION

Assessing the current situation with your technology gives you a starting point. You have to know what you have, why you have it, and how everyone feels about it before you can make a plan to move forward.

DEFINE USE CASES

First, define the use cases. A use case can be any business objective you're trying to accomplish. When you define a use case, instead of focusing on the features and functionality of the technology, first think about what your people are actually trying to do and what they have to do to accomplish the task.

Within a marketing automation platform, for example, a use case might be sending a trigger-based email when a prospect takes a particular action. Maybe they interacted with the website in a way that identifies them to us as someone in our target audience. How does a marketing person interact with this scenario? What do they need to do to execute this task successfully? Other common use cases include automating lead qualifications, event follow-up, and reporting and analytics around departmental initiatives. Each of these cases often involves some tech and a lot of manual processes that might be replaced with technology, or better technology.

CREATE A MATRIX AND IDENTIFY GAPS AND OVERLAPS

Once you've defined all your use cases, create a matrix of the technologies used to satisfy each one and the business objective they solve. The matrix shows you which technologies are actually in use. It will also show you where there is overlap and where gaps exist. If you own technology that no one uses, are you still paying for licenses? Are you paying an annual maintenance agreement? Should you hang onto the technology or decommission it? Overlapping technologies are those that can be used to satisfy the same business objectives. Why are you paying for two when one does the job? A gap in technology appears where you satisfy a use case with tech that isn't a good fit. A common example is an email marketing platform that doesn't integrate with webinar platforms. As a result, deploying webinars requires a lot of manual processes. If your company runs a lot of online events, this is an obvious pain point and a perfect opportunity to look at other email marketing platforms to satisfy the business objective. Another gap is where a use case isn't resolved by technology at all but entirely by manual process. Is there an opportunity to automate the process with existing or new technology?

GAPS THAT KILL (REVENUE)

A few years ago, a manufacturer rolled out a membership program. Customers who opted in received a special card in the mail identifying them as members and giving them discounts on purchases, along with other benefits.

The business didn't think through the use case of the program and were doing everything manually. When a customer signed up, they sent them an email notifying them that their membership request had been accepted. Then they printed out a certificate identifying the customer as a card-carrying member of the "club." They had cards made up with the company logo and each person's name, which they had to mail out along with the certificates. As they went through this process, they had to update the CRM system to identify the members, mark them as eligible for discounted pricing, and make sure they were notified of other options.

We worked with them to lay out the use case with their manual process—then we tallied up their investment in the program. All that data input, printing, and mailing had cost them $100,000 in people hours! We showed them a technology to automate the process, saving them time and money and ensuring a consistent customer experience. Needless to say, it wasn't hard for them to pull the trigger on that decision.

Technology gaps can be extremely expensive. Doing things manually may seem like a simple solution, but when you take a closer look, you may find you're shooting yourself in the foot.

TEAM SENTIMENT

So far, this is pretty straightforward. But let's not forget about your internal end users. The final piece of the technology assessment and validation is "team sentiment." Often overlooked, how past and current users actually *feel* about the technology should be considered. Do they love it? Do they hate it? Are they indifferent about it? If it went away, how would people feel? If someone says they absolutely love a tool, that's a good indicator. If they have to use it, but either don't like it or don't really feel one way or another about it, you may want to look for a different tool that solves the problem.

TECHNOLOGY SELECTION

The matrix showed you all the gaps and overlaps. Next, you have to decide what to do about them. Making your use cases more effective and efficient usually requires getting rid of tech you don't use or where there's overlap, using currently unused features of tech you already own to replace tech that no one loves, and buying some new tech to replace the bad and fill in the gaps.

GO WITH A PRO

Before you start shopping, let's be crystal clear about one thing: most people do not know how to select the right technology for their use cases. This isn't a slam against department heads; it's just a fact. There is a lot of technology out there, and every vendor will have you believe theirs is the best. If you take just one piece of advice away from this whole book, it's this: You spend less than 1 percent of your time under the hood of all the different technologies. Leverage someone that spends *most* of their time under the hood and most of their time connecting an extreme level of technical detail to use cases. Leave your ego at the door for this one. When it comes to making a tech purchase, get professional help.

> If you take just one piece of advice away from this whole book, it's this: You spend less than 1 percent of your time under the hood of all the different technologies. Leverage someone that spends *most* of their time under the hood and most of their time connecting an extreme level of technical detail to use cases. Leave your ego at the door for this one. When it comes to making a tech purchase, get professional help.

Technically, you can evaluate and purchase your own technology. But there is a heavy cost associated with getting it wrong. Think of it this way: If your Tesla broke down on the side of the road, would you get out your toolkit and try to fix it? Would you start tinkering under the hood with your screwdriver? Or would you call a tow truck, then your mechanic, to take care of it for you? Whichever route you go, someone will have to deal with the consequences of your decisions.

Free online resources like G2 Crowd can help you learn

about different technologies. If you're starting to shop around, check out their analyses and reviews to get a feel for what's available, what might fit, and what probably won't. Then hire someone to learn your environment and needs and direct you to the best solution.

Introducing a new product to your technology stack can be labor-intensive. There's always a learning curve, process refinements, and trickle-down effects. The implementation and execution can go smoothly, or be very, very painful. The benefit of hiring a professional technologist to step through the details of how the right tech solves a use case and operates within your environment outweighs the cost of getting it wrong.

We feel strongly about this because we're consultants in the business, and we've seen homegrown implementations go very, very wrong. Companies that try to do this on their own end up wasting a lot of time and money before they realize they need a professional to help them out. By that time, a year or longer has passed. Hiring a consultant could have streamlined the process and put it into action, and the company could be enjoying the benefits.

YOU DON'T ALWAYS NEED "BEST IN CLASS"

It's perfectly okay to *not* choose the best-in-class product. Technology that's less popular and more niche than what "everyone else" is using could be a great choice for you. It may have a smaller user base and limited functionality, but if it does exactly what you need, it could be the perfect tech for you. It could have a smaller footprint and require little or no customization. You could become a valuable customer to the vendor because you're aligned with what they do best, which encourages better support.

FOCUS ON FUNCTIONALITY

While we're here, we want to let you in on a little secret: Vendors like to wave their products' shiny new features and functions around. They like to talk about what they have that the competition doesn't. They expect you to get excited about features that don't matter to you, not because those features satisfy your use cases (they usually don't) but because they like to prey on your fear of missing out. So they might add a little AI here or a little account-based marketing (ABM) there. During your initial research, focus on the functionality that matters most for your desired outcome, not the bells and whistles. Do you need AI or ABM for the use case you're solving? Will it do anything for the associated business initiative? If the answer is no, then you don't need it. And you should not pay for it. If all that fancy stuff doesn't satisfy the use case you're buying it for, then WHY DO YOU EVEN CARE? It's not going to help you. Shut that stuff down fast. Don't be distracted. Save your money and throw your team a party to celebrate your smart tech purchase instead.

VALIDATE THE FUNCTIONALITY

Shocking news alert: do not take the salesperson's word about what their tech can do. We've heard it all, including claims similar to "You can turn this baby on, walk away, and it will do everything for you." What a value proposition! I'll take ten of those.

Validate the functionality. Don't skip this part in either your technology purchase decision *or* in this chapter. Read the rest of this because it's important AND not as obvious or simple as you might think. We'll go out on a limb here and proclaim that validating the functionality is *complicated*. Again, this is why you might need the outside help of a professional technology consultant. The technology might be "good enough" for your needs, but other options could be a lot better.

Work with your technologist to identify and prioritize what you need the technology to do. Then you can make a head-to-head comparison and methodically decide which product meets the most needs and is the best at addressing your most important priorities.

Before you make a final decision, request proof of concept. Bring the product in-house to validate that it does what it promises. Does it do the job? Does it do it well? Is it easy to use, or is there a lot of manual intervention involved? How does it work with your other tech? What's the learning curve like? Does it have the flexibility to handle your use cases that vary beyond the norm from time to time? Involve the end users in the proof of concept and get their feedback. This is critical because when you build use cases, people will forget that they need certain functionalities in a product, but when they actually use it, they'll remember. During a proof of concept, they might also find that a technology provides much better results than whatever they've been using. As improved methods and outcomes come to light, you may end up redefining your requirements.

During this proof of concept phase, you'll find that some technologies have native functionality that meets your needs, though a better choice may be technology with the flexibility to support unique use cases. A best-in-class marketing automation platform supports a wide variety of use cases effectively. Content experience platforms and social tools with some flexibility that allows you to stretch them beyond your typical use cases may be a good choice, depending on your needs. Again, don't dismiss lesser-known technologies that do the job and do it well. But look at those that do more, too, supporting more use cases or fulfilling a future need.

Choosing the right tech is a science, but it's also an art, and the right choice is not the same for every business or operation—yet another reason to seriously consider hiring a technologist to help you with these decisions. They're more aware of what's out there, practiced at research, and unbiased. They don't buy into the hype around new technologies and will not choose some tech because the vendor happens to be a really nice guy who brings you bagels. If you tell them, "I need an email marketing platform that supports this unique use case," a technologist will take the research off your hands and land on a solution much faster because they live and breathe technology every day. It's what they do.

IMPLEMENTATION, INTEGRATION, AND OPTIMIZATION

After you've made a purchase, you have to install it, get it to work with your other tech, and tweak it to do its job really well. A successful implementation starts with a strong strategy. Do not skip this step (in blinking letters). Really, don't.

Whether the implementation is a heavy lift or plug and play, bringing any new tech into your ecosystem requires a clear understanding of how it fits into the big picture of what the organization is trying to accomplish. Think about how it will impact the customer experience and how it will achieve the desired result. Consider how it integrates with other tech and how that affects the customer experience. Understand the role it plays in the big picture and how other tech might support it in that role.

For example, a marketing automation tool may need to be connected to the CRM system to do its job. So you will have to look at the flow of data: what's getting pulled from the CRM or pushed from the CRM, and how does that happen? The systems need to talk to each other for your new tech to satisfy the use cases you bought it for.

When you're thinking strategy, focus on the big picture functionality and flow and how that affects the outcome. That should be your focus—not the nuts and bolts of "How do we get this thing up and running?" That will come later, but if your focus is on that piece initially, you will miss the opportunity to build a holistic solution that gets you where you need to be with the customer experience.

Create a plan for rolling out the tech so that on Day 1, you are using some of the functionality. You might not be able to address every use case immediately, but work up to it, tweaking as you go until you are using all the functionality you need. Also, have a plan for growth so that as your needs change, the functionality scales. Over time, your business objectives and use cases will evolve. The technology should flex within the tech stack to meet that evolution and growth. Optimize the implementation to get the full value out of your purchase.

YOU'VE MADE IT THIS FAR...

The Revenue Takeover is a four-phase process, but you will see incremental results after completing each step. We typically expect to see, on the *low* end, a 10 percent improvement in metrics, including performance, profitability, and engagement, in businesses that complete Phase 1. Simply having the right technologies in place drives growth. If this step doesn't do that for you, reexamine your business objectives to ensure they are in line with an improved customer experience.

You know that technology is key to your business and revenue. By now, you've seen why trusting technology purchase decisions to anyone other than a specialist doesn't make sense. Bringing in a technologist is the smart path, but you don't have to stop there. Once you've got the right tech, someone has to run it. To maintain that high-level view and holistic approach you applied in your tech strategy, you need a team that shares that same vision. You need people who are focused solely on the tech and how it all works together to make your customers the happiest people on Earth. Or at least happier than they are now, and definitely happier than the competition's customers.

The decisions and resources you need to complete Phase 1 are within your control. You might interact with other departments, but for the most part, you can get this step done without a lot of buy-in from others. In the next phase, you'll step outside your sphere of influence. You will need the support of your leadership and colleagues.

You will also need people who see the big picture and have the technical expertise to make it happen. You probably interacted with people like this during Phase 1—people who didn't just do as they were told, but who shared your holistic vision. Keep these people in mind. They could play a bigger role in Phase 2.

At this point in the Revenue Takeover, you're 25 percent of the way there. You are seeing an improvement, and you may be tempted to sit back, enjoy the success, and quit here. Or you could keep going because the results will be more dramatic in Phases 2, 3, and 4. They're going to blow your mind.

CHAPTER 13

BUILDING REVOPS

It takes ten times as long to put yourself back together as it does to fall apart.

—SUZANNE COLLINS

The Head of Marketing has control over the marketing department and some of the technology it uses to accomplish goals. Making better decisions about the tech you purchase is the first step toward leveraging technology to optimize the customer experience, which in turn drives revenue. The next step isn't so easy, but it's essential to getting all the technology that influences your customers' perception of the business aligned.

In this step, you have to expand your sphere of influence to technology, processes, and all things customer-related that are presently *not* under your command. For that to happen, the organizational structure has to change. We warned you—this is major. It's a huge shift in how customer experience strategies are envisioned and executed. It's a shift in how marketing operates. It's a shift in who does the work. It seems risky, right? Why would you want to change something that's been working so well for so long?

Because it hasn't been working that well. Not nearly as well as it could. Accomplishing Phase 1 of the Revenue Takeover only gets you partway there. We've seen companies stop at that phase, and we've seen others take the next step. Those that move forward to manage and control the processes, people, and technology of the Modern Front Office see greater velocity on the path to improving customer experience and driving revenue.

Growing your influence by taking control over aspects of the business that you don't currently own—and probably don't fully understand—might sound scary. In a sense, you really are proposing a "takeover." If this sounds like a war tactic, it sort of is: You are going to take the best players from several teams and put them on your team. You may have to hire some ringers to round out the team. You may decide you're not the best coach for the team, too. We'll get to that later. For now, understand that you are going to reshape the organizational structure and how the Modern Front Office's Revenue Team functions. You're planning a takeover, but it's a friendly takeover where everyone wins, and nobody gets hurt.

As a wise king once said, "So it begins."

THE RIGHT PLAYERS

You have a lot of teams supporting the tech that supports revenue: Sales Operations, Marketing Operations, IT, Customer Support. You might have more, and the names might vary. The goal here is to bring the right players from each team onto *one* team—a new team called RevOps. This team's priority is the technology that supports the customer experience.

REVOPS FORMING

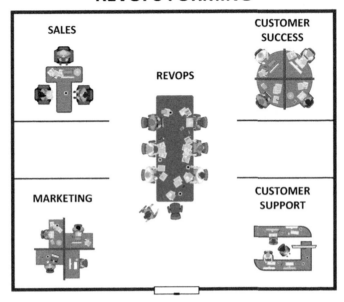

Technology responsibilities in the Modern Front Office are consolidated into one holistic team. This new RevOps team manages the tech stack for the many functions, bringing together formerly separate teams to achieve shared initiatives.

The team comprises individuals from several departments, but these people are coming together to form their own team. They aren't just reorganized under a new name or in a different area of the building, retaining their same roles and responsibilities. They each bring a skillset to the team that contributes to the priority and the goal of managing and leveraging the technology that supports the customer experience. The creation of RevOps is the first step toward seeing the Modern Front Office, the technology that supports it, and the entire customer journey holistically, instead of from the view of each individual department and team.

The people of RevOps change their team, and their roles, and their titles. A director of sales operations who moves to RevOps might become the director of revenue operations. Each person is reassigned and given a new directive. The creation of the team has to be formalized. It's not a casual change in how things are run. It's major, like all the Power Rangers putting their Zords together to form the Megazord. And just like the Power Rangers, RevOps needs a leader to ensure interconnectedness among the technology, tools, and functions of the team.

GET BUY-IN STARTING FROM THE TOP

To influence organizational change outside of your current circle, you have to get buy-in from everyone involved and affected, starting with the CEO. If leadership isn't on board, you won't achieve RevOps' goals. The CMO—or CRO— can't send a memo to HR declaring, "Hey, we just started a new department. Can you order us some new nameplates for our cubes and offices? And while you're at it, go ahead and change the org chart."

Paint the picture of the future to the CEO. Help them see your vision. You want this person to see the entire picture, not just a piece of it, so they see where you're going with

RevOps. You need their immediate buy-in on building a RevOps team.

We're going to show you an example of RevOps, but the details vary depending on the business. If you're moving forward with your Revenue Takeover, hold off on your conversation with the CEO until you've finished the book. There is more to this vision, and once you have the whole picture, it will be easier to explain the possible future for the company.

They may not sign off on the whole vision initially, and that's okay. It's a lot. But if you show them the possibilities and ask them for the go-ahead on this one piece, you'll have a chance to prove what a difference a team committed to revenue operations can make. Prepare for that conversation. Have your bullet points in your head and be ready to lay them out:

- More efficiency. RevOps will have an overall view of your customer experience resources and technology, so you won't be buying tech that doesn't work with, or that overlaps, the tech you already own. They are the technology experts and will be focused on buying what makes the most sense for your customer experience goals.
- Increased productivity. RevOps will take care of the technology that touches the customer so your Market-

ing, Sales, Support, and Success people can focus on what they were hired to do.

- A holistic view into how the customer experience impacts revenue. One team pulling reports and doing analysis on data instead of several teams doing that work and then trying to make sense of the different numbers.
- Aside from your IT department and perhaps other departments such as engineering that may have their own technology budgets, just one RevTech budget to deal with.
- Instead of a disjointed customer experience, an optimized one with consistent branding, messaging, and interactions that promote more sales.
- Customer retention, which in time can lead to increased profits and higher revenue.
- A better culture and happier employees. They would be working toward shared goals and have greater visibility into how their activities affect other departments and vice versa. They would also see how their work contributes to the bottom line and realize their importance to the company's success.

FORMING THE REVOPS TEAM

RevOps takes care of evaluating, purchasing, and implementing technologies. Under their leader's guidance, they are tasked with making sure the technology fully supports the customer experience in a way that makes sense for the business.

The RevOps team might comprise individuals from Marketing, Sales, Support, and Success. For example, if you currently have two people in Marketing managing marketing ops, three in Sales taking care of sales ops, and one tech person in Support, you could pull those people onto one team to form your revenue operations team. Other than these six people that would now form their own team, Marketing, Sales, Support, and Success would remain intact and continue to report to their current leadership. We are simply adding a fifth department—RevOps—to manage all the technology that the other functions use to create and enhance the customer experience.

The RevOps executive leader should be familiar with revenue and operations. They should be a strategist and a technologist. They must work alongside other leaders in the company and be responsible for identifying technological opportunities to support the customer experience. They will have to work arm-in-arm with the other revenue leaders such as the heads of Marketing, Sales, Support, and Success to understand the overarching strategy of those functions. This is necessary for RevOps to ensure technology that supports the customer experience strategy end-to-end. The leader would oversee the RevOps team and its operations, and with the advantage of visibility into the other functions' strategies, would develop a holistic strategy for all Modern Front Office technology used by Marketing, Sales, Success, and Support.

A common error at this point is hiring or promoting a strictly technical person into this role who has zero strategy in their bones. Your main expert on CRM, or your database whiz, is not the person for the job. You need someone with technical knowledge who also has the skills to lead Marketing and Sales. The person should be respected as a leader, and not just as a technologist.

Key to the RevOps leader's success is their mastery of strategy. They have to know how all the pieces fit together and how they support the customer experience. They need enough technical knowledge to manage a team of technologists. They must also understand the reason for RevOps: its purpose and mission. This takes a special kind of person with a broad skillset. Remember, beyond the technology and knowledge of customer experience, they will be leading a brand-new team. The person must have superior leadership abilities.

You might have someone who fills this role perfectly, or who could with some training. If you don't, consider a new hire. Don't just put anyone in this position, or you may be setting them and the whole RevOps team up for failure.

THIS DOES NOT LOOK THE SAME FOR EVERYONE

Some companies have, within their various customer experience teams, discrete technology and operations teams. Marketing might have a marketing ops person, and Sales might have a sales ops person, for example. Other businesses rely on IT for all their marketing technology and operations needs. Still other companies blur the line between who owns what as far as technology, with different departments owning different pieces of the tech. Finally, it's not uncommon for a business to have "shadow" teams that, much like shadow IT, purchase technology to fill a specific need without disclosing what they're doing or why to other teams that may be impacted.

A prime example of this is a business we worked with where their marketing ops team owned all the technology for demand generation and campaign execution, but IT owned integrations. The point here is that every company does tech differently, so before you institute a RevOps team, you have to figure out where you currently stand.

Think about what happens when you've tried to integrate two marketing systems. Who bought the tech, and who did the integration? Consider how these kinds of projects are currently managed, and you should be able to pick apart who owns the pieces and what happens with those pieces as far as purchasing, integration, support, and decommissioning. Who does the paperwork on this stuff?

The more convoluted your current structure, the tougher it might be to move to RevOps. If you have clear lines, it could be a fairly simple move. You know who owns the technology, and they are the obvious people to move into RevOps. When the lines are blurred—for instance, a marketing manager owns marketing for a specific function like lead gen and also manages the tech for marketing—the move could be more difficult. You are essentially taking the tech responsibilities off that person's plate and handing them to someone else. Alternatively, that marketing manager may be a great candidate for RevOps team leader. Where you start from will affect where you end up and how long it takes to get there.

Occasionally, a leader who's asked to relinquish control over technology will balk at the idea. More often, they will jump for joy, delighted that someone is able and willing to take on the job, freeing them to do what they're best at: Marketing, Sales, Support, or Success.

You might catch flak from IT too, or at least get a lot of questions—especially if you're taking tech off their plate that they've integrated and have been supporting. An easy way to distinguish what IT keeps and what they give up is to answer the question: does it touch the customer? If the answer is yes, it's RevOps' baby. If no, then it's back-office technology, and IT should hang onto it.

The IT manager should support this, knowing that RevOps

has already been immersed in technology. The heads of the functions within your Revenue Team should also embrace the switch since the people in RevOps know what Sales, Marketing, Support, and Success are doing. Bringing the tech teams together to ensure end-to-end support should make those leaders incredibly happy.

There will be points of contact for IT's and RevOps' technology. In a company where sales data from a CRM system flows into an ERP system, with RevOps managing the CRM and IT owning the ERP, the teams will have to collaborate to ensure data integrity and flow. Other considerations in this scenario include security. If IT owns security standards regarding purchasing decisions, RevOps must comply with those, and IT may need to validate any tech purchases.

As different technology owners wade into the RevOps waters, a team charter or mandate should be discussed, agreed upon, and documented. This states who owns the different technologies and who supports them. It stipulates their working relationship, especially where there is overlap or dependencies. The document should state how teams work together to accomplish their own goals and the company's goals.

THE TEAM HAS TO BE FRONT AND CENTER

RevOps must be highly visible. They cannot operate like

shadow IT. They are essentially supporting the Revenue Team, and there can be no barriers around what they are doing. They need to be front and center, involved in the tech decisions, and seen as a key resource for the Modern Front Office.

This is where RevOps really differs from traditional IT. Where Information Technology tends to operate "out of the way," it is often seen as secretive, in a way, communicating with the people it supports on a need-to-know basis. RevOps needs to be more accessible to, and communicative with, its end users.

This transparency goes both ways. The people RevOps supports must also be open about the tools they use and what they do so that RevOps can support the customer experience holistically. Depending on the size of your business and the skills of your team, the RevOps team would interact with other functions within the Revenue Team to include a certain amount of cross-training and job shadowing so they fully understand the day-to-day workings of each department and what people are trying to achieve.

MAKE IT REAL

The formation of RevOps requires a shift in the way people see how they fit in the company. Promote this transformation by making it "real." Move people out of their cubicles and offices and into a new area so RevOps is sitting together. Give them new titles and new job descriptions. Provide the leadership they need to give them direction. They will still be interacting with their old teammates, but in a different way. They have a new leader, new goals, and a new way of seeing how they support the teams and tech that interact with customers and the organization as a whole. Make it official. This could mean some kind of ceremonial gesture—taking them off-site to talk about who they are, what they are doing, and how that impacts the business. They have been chosen for this new role because they are uniquely qualified in some way, and while that has to be recognized, they must also understand the responsibility that comes with it. They are RevOps—committed to the customer experience and the revenue that comes from delivering on that goal.

WHAT FORMING THE TEAM LOOKS LIKE

You will have new reporting lines. People will be moved onto this new team with a new leader. The team has its own budget. How this team supports the Modern Front Office will be all new too. The old marketing operations person is now a RevOps person, working alongside the old sales ops person, for instance. They are no longer focused solely on their old departments but on supporting all of the teams as a whole.

If a marketing manager says to the old ops technician, "Hey, we need to start tracking this new dataset in our marketing automation platform," the technician who is now part of RevOps doesn't look at that task as a marketing request. They have to take into account how it impacts all the other teams and the technology they use. In fact, there has to be a new process for how the request comes in and is validated to ensure it aligns with the RevOps strategy. This can create some confusion initially because the department heads are used to having their technology or operations people do what they're asked, and now there is another layer that they will have to go through to make sure what they're asking makes sense for the customer experience and all the other teams that support it.

RevOps can head off these issues by instituting a responsive intake process for requests. After all, they are a services organization, and the teams they support are their internal customers. But if the strategy is well-defined and communicated to the department heads, and everyone has buy-in, then there should be an understanding that RevOps' priorities are in line with serving the internal customer so those people can better serve the external one, thereby creating an optimized customer experience and generating more revenue. Make that vision clear to everyone. Repeat it as often as you need to. But also be transparent and responsive. If a request doesn't align with the strategy, explain why: it's not because you're too busy or don't want to do the work—it's because the request is out of sync with what you all agreed to, and instead of pulling you toward the Revenue Team's goals, it uses resources to take you away from them.

If RevOps fails to get the buy-in from Marketing, Sales, Support, and Success, those other teams may be tempted to create their own shadow groups to work around RevOps, defeating the purpose of the team's creation and undermining the customer experience.

TALENT GAPS AND OVERLAPS

As you pull people from teams to create RevOps, you'll find gaps. It turns out the Sales Ops technician didn't just manage the tech and operations for Sales, they were also writing a weekly blog for prospects. They're not going to be doing that in RevOps, so now you have to task someone else with the job or create a new role to fill. You may have to hire someone. You may need to hire new people for RevOps too. This will take some time, and the talent gaps will reveal themselves. There may be overlap too. You could have two people who were previously doing the same job for their respective departments, and now you only need one person for that job in RevOps. All this needs to be considered as you form the new team.

Over time, you'll figure out who fits in RevOps and who does not. Personalities are definitely part of the mix, and some people work very well in a narrow, focused position where they are handed a task and they do it without questioning whether it makes sense. On the RevOps team, that kind of thinking doesn't fly. People will have to see the bigger picture and be willing to question a request before they take it on. Not everyone is wired to work this way, and within a few months of RevOps' formation, people may decide they're not cut out for it. Or the leader may have to make that decision for them.

A LAYERED APPROACH

RevOps' leader and the team have two layers: strategic and tactical. The tactical piece ensures day-to-day execution, efficiency, and technical expertise. The strategic piece looks at the bigger picture to ensure the technology and the work make sense for the customer experience.

Technology makes the strategy possible, but it does not drive it. The RevOps leader, with the help of the team, looks at all the tech that impacts the customer experience. They see these technologies holistically and assess whether they are having the desired effect. They may have to revisit the marketplace to find other products to achieve the desired outcome. Some of the technology will be replaced, and new tech may be required. You may find tech that can go away completely. The strategy looks at the customer experience first, and by enhancing that, the tech and the work become more efficient. Ultimately, the goal is to drive revenue—not from a transaction standpoint but from the belief that a better customer experience leads to faster sales and more revenue.

REVOPS' FIRST OBJECTIVE

RevOps doesn't throw out all the current technology and start from scratch. Their first job is to assess what they have. Remember, in Phase 1, Marketing went through this process. In Phase 2, RevOps takes over that process and completes it across all technologies for the departments it supports—the Revenue Team comprising Marketing, Sales, Support, and Success, which make up the Modern Front Office.

Using the strategic objectives as their North Star, RevOps defines the future of the technology: what they need to achieve those objectives, how it interfaces with other technology and the internal user, and how it interfaces with the customer. This step involves people from the strategic and tactical sides of RevOps. Together, they create a blueprint for the future of technology and the customer experience. Every company's objectives may be different, but they all have to start here.

RevOps defines the future of the technology: what they need to achieve those objectives, how it interfaces with other technology and the internal user, and how it interfaces with the customer.

CHALLENGES AND SOLUTIONS

Some companies will find the shift to RevOps challenging or just not possible in their immediate future. The best time to do it may be when you're already making changes—during new hire initiatives or layoffs. If you are going to make sweeping changes, get it right and do it all at once. Otherwise, you may find yourself having to initiate a Revenue Takeover five years from now just to compete, and it will be a lot harder, and you will have lost precious years when you could have been fine-tuning the process.

Some companies may choose to hire a third party to manage the Revenue Takeover. Consultants can step them through the process and be as involved or as hands-off as the business wants and needs them to be. The third party can bring in their own RevOps team, or they can collaborate across existing departments to help them work together in a more holistic way. They can also help the company develop a strategic and tactical plan, move or hire the right people to create the RevOps team, and coach them to the point that they're ready to manage the work on their own. In other words, you don't have to do a total re-org to reap the benefits. You can move toward a Revenue Takeover in steps and with outside guidance.

Bringing in a third party also brings in the expertise of people who have "done it" before and are familiar with the problems you need to solve. They have dealt with the same or similar problems at other companies. They have tech expertise, too, and have most likely worked with many more technologies than the people on your current staff. A consultant will be more objective and less personally attached to the project because they are not vested in trying to wrestle control away from one department or another, or trying to make one department look like the hero and the rest look like losers that need rescuing. They look at all the departments, and all the tech, and how it all works together.

If you do bring in a third party, you might also want them to help manage the knowledge around the technology. When a person leaves a business, they take what they know with them. Unless every process is documented and you have redundancy in talent and training, there will be a gap while you try to figure out what that person did, who will do it now, and how they will do it. Creating and managing RevOps' technical knowledge base, including documentation of processes, can be managed in-house or hired out. This is especially important for companies going through down-sizing events, where internal knowledge is often lost.

A good third-party RevOps team or consultant will focus on objectives, obstacles, and solutions. They don't make anyone out to be the good guy or bad guy—they just say, "this is good" or "this is bad," and employees deal with the facts in their own way. Whether they involve company politics or start blaming each other is not a factor in a good consultant's perspective of what really is good or bad.

If you decide to go this route, look for a third party that specializes in revenue technology consulting. If they do only IT, or only marketing, sales, customer support, or success tech, they will not understand the whole picture.

THE CUSTOMER WINS

The real winner in this process is the customer. They get a more cohesive experience with your business from beginning to end. That, in turn, leads to faster sales, more sales, and increased revenue.

You may not get any feedback at all about the improvements from your customer base. They'll just feel better about buying from you and probably won't even know why. The changes may be so subtle that even your regular customers won't be able to articulate why it's easier, and better, and more enjoyable to buy from you. But it will be, and in time, the difference will be apparent in how your teams work together, in how much more efficiently your technology works together, and ultimately, in sales.

In Phase 1, we talked about reevaluating the technology and lining up behind the tech. In Phase 2, we created a team specifically tasked with taking on the strategy and tactical execution of managing the technology. In Phase 3, we'll step away from the tech. This is where you get more into the people and processes that make the Revenue Takeover a wild success.

CHAPTER 14

WHAT REAL CHANGE LOOKS LIKE

Amateurs sit and wait for inspiration, the rest of us just get up and go to work.

—STEPHEN KING

At this point, some of your people have coalesced into this new team, RevOps. Others remain in Marketing, Sales, Service, and Success. Whichever team they're on, they won't really know how their roles have changed or make the connection between the work they do and revenue. Jack in Support will still think he's closing a certain number of support tickets in a certain amount of time to hit a goal. Niesha in Marketing will still believe she's writing a set number of social media posts to fill an editorial calendar.

You have to show them how what they do impacts revenue in the Revenue Takeover. You do this with a cohesive plan that crosses department barriers to focus on organizational revenue targets, a Revenue Team and Modern Front Office to meet those targets, and functional and personal goals to optimize the customer experience. The plan is not done by department. That defeats the purpose. It's *holistic*. Each individual and each department plays an important part in the change.

A lot of leaders have tried to initiate a change that brings the results of a Revenue Takeover. They have the best intentions and are hopeful that they can make it work. Leaders understand the value of coming together and using that synergy to collaborate on objectives that serve the company's goals. But at some point, their efforts fall short and the whole plan begins to erode. Eventually, it falls apart. People drift back into the same patterns of behavior and work that they've been doing—the work they're comfortable doing.

Change is hard. It's not impossible. And it's a lot easier when you have momentum in your favor. The incremental changes you make and actions you take in earlier phases *create* the momentum necessary to succeed. You're taking steps and experiencing efficiency and growth, so it's easier to continue taking steps. Then you're ready for the next big step: changing the way you talk about "why you work."

What do we mean by changing the way you talk? Well, consider Bob. He used to be on the Sales Ops team. Bob's a superstar, and now he's on the RevOps team. When he was in Sales Ops, Bob focused on his tasks, and he was good at them. But that's what they were to him—tasks. He didn't see the big picture and how his tasks contributed to the company's goals. He didn't understand how what he does affects revenue. He didn't see Molly over in Marketing or Syd over in Support as part of his team. Now Molly and Bob are on the same team—RevOps. Working side-by-side opens the door to greater visibility, communication, and understanding. Bob sees how the two of them, working together, make a bigger contribution to the business than they did as individuals. Bob's measured differently now, too, and he's starting to see how his work contributes to each function in the Modern Front Office. Eventually, Bob might see how his work impacts revenue.

Bob's job isn't just a job anymore. He has a purpose. He has an important role in the success of the company that depends on him helping other people do their jobs better to ensure a better experience for the customer to ensure more revenue. That's a good thing for everyone. Bob isn't selling anything, by the way. He hasn't joined the salesforce, but he is doing what the company needs him to do to meet its revenue goals.

OVERARCHING SHARED GOALS

The first step in this phase is a strategic collaboration around shared goals, but not just any goal. Choose three *Wildly Important Goals*, or "WIGs." A WIG is so wildly important that failing to achieve it would make any other success seem secondary. WIGs have a finish line that can be defined as "getting from X to Y by Z," where X is the current state, Y signals achievement of the goal, and Z is the timeframe. An example of a Wildly Important Goal around moving the needle on revenue is "Going from 2 million to 4 million in 18 months." The timeframe can be the end of a month, quarter, year...whatever you need it to be, with consideration for resources, workforce, how quickly your company can shift gears, and how aggressively the company wants to move.

Each WIG cannot be achievable by a single function. Everyone in the Modern Front Office should be included in the work involved. The goals cannot be achieved by each function *individually* either. In other words, a goal like "Meeting Your Department's Goals on Time and Under Budget" supports the culture we need to dissolve. Every team's contributions are necessary to meet the three WIGs.

These three WIGs become the *top* priorities for each department. They will have other goals beyond the WIGs, and some may impact the Wildly Important Goals. But these three goals will always be front and center and not something a function gets around to after they've done all their other work. To ensure that each function's focus remains on the WIGs, we recommend tying the head of each department's compensation to WIG success. The Head of Success's quarterly bonus, for example, relies on their department's successful contributions to the three WIGs.

The WIGs aren't developed in a vacuum and assigned to departments. The heads of each of the five functions will need to come together to agree on goals they are willing to support and believe best serve the business's objectives. The leader of this initiative should discuss the goals as follows:

1. Individually, in one-on-one conversations with each executive
2. Then at an off-site meeting with all the executives together
3. Post off-sites individually, with each executive
4. Finally, the executives will commence planning with their respective teams

You can jumpstart the process on your own with these steps:

1. Outline the overarching organizational goals, specifically those relative to customer experience and/or revenue.
2. Assuming you are the Head of Marketing, meet with

the heads of Sales, Success, Support, and RevOps and document each function's current goals and priorities as well as your own.

3. Block out your calendar for a day or two—longer if you need it—to identify opportunities for synergy between the departmental goals.

OUTLINE OVERARCHING ORGANIZATIONAL GOALS

You should have access to the company's annual goals on your internal site and through discussions with your CEO. It's the kind of information presented at all-hands meetings, and if you're in a leadership position, you're probably reminded of these goals in executive meetings.

These goals are not the mission statement, vision statement, or guiding principles. They are goals the CEO and the executive team are striving to accomplish within a set timeframe, so in your research, look for goals with a targeted deadline. Those related to customer experience or revenue are more likely to be in the five teams' wheelhouses, so you might want to focus on those first, but don't automatically exclude a goal if you don't see a connection immediately.

These goals may or may not have a metric. For example, "Increase revenue by 20 percent" is pretty clear. "Reestablish the brand and regain position as a leader in the space" is not. It's broad, but if you can establish a metric that signifies "leadership in the space," you can create a WIG for that goal.

DOCUMENT CURRENT GOALS AND PRIORITIES

Document the current goals and priorities of your Revenue Team—the departments such as Marketing, Sales, Support, and Success that make up the Modern Front Office—and include RevOps. Remember, these people and their work have the most direct effect on customer experience. Your company may have more or fewer teams that fit this category, and the teams could have different names.

From here, you need to figure out which of these goals have the greatest impact on the organizational goals. Each function is already contributing to those goals, and so their priorities will likely already be lined up with them. From the earlier example, if a business's goal is to reestablish the brand and regain position as a leader in the space, Marketing, Sales, and the other functions will have departmental goals in place to assist with that broader goal.

Talk to the heads of each department. If the connection between what they're doing and the company's goals isn't clear, ask them to explain it to you. That connection may be obvious to them but not to you. For example, priorities like "call resolution" and "time to response" make perfect sense to Support or Success in their efforts to regain position, but you may need more information to understand how those goals affect positioning.

IDENTIFY OPPORTUNITIES FOR SYNERGY

The goal in this step is to identify the current goals within the Modern Front Office departments that, combined, could have a dramatic enough impact on the organization's revenue to qualify as a WIG. You might find synergy between goals like signing renewals and driving "stickiness" where you're selling more to current customers. The synergy could be around Net Promoter scores or a measurable metric of customer experience. Again, you can separate the goals into two lists: those that have the potential for synergy and those that do not. You will find that some functions are already doing a lot to impact revenue while others are not.

It's important that you do this work upfront. This shows that you're committed to the project and gives everyone some direction. Otherwise, when you get into the planning stage, the conversation could be unproductive as each person rallies to promote initiatives where they are already succeeding or that they are already hyper-focused around. The synergy is *critically* important, and so you have to show that to everyone immediately.

Start the work on your own, but don't finish it alone. Get together with the other department heads and tell them,

"This is our starting point. Let's talk about where we go from here." When you schedule that meeting, be clear about your expectations and the desired outcome: to agree on three Wildly Important Goals that support the company's goals by enhancing the customer experience to generate revenue. Expect each conversation to take at least half a day. This is not a superficial introduction to the concept of WIGs; it's a "We're going to hash it out until we're done" meeting. You might plan an all-day off-site for this, so people aren't distracted.

Depending on the size of your business and how well the leadership works together, you may not be able to accomplish this in one sitting. In that case, schedule four half-days four weeks in a row or an all-day meeting every quarter to establish the WIGs and discuss progress. Short meetings of an hour or so won't cut it. Each sit-down has to be long enough and without interruption to do the deep work toward real progress.

Ask for their feedback on what you got right and what you misunderstood in your interpretation of their priorities and goals. Give everyone ample time to talk and listen carefully to what they have to say. At this point, you are the expert in the room regarding the development of three Wildly Important Goals, but you will need their knowledge to get it right.

Expect this conversation to be enlightening. It's natural to be focused on your own work and have little insight into what your colleagues are trying to accomplish. This step is where the barriers really start to come down. People who once thought theirs was the only department involved in revenue generation are going to see others in a new light. The transparency will promote a new understanding and perhaps a fresh attitude among your peers. You will each have a clearer picture of how each team is already working toward many of the same goals. This in itself will help to decompress the pressure people feel to achieve their department goals because they will realize that they are not alone. Others are working toward the same larger goal, and though they may have never realized this fact before, they are all in this together.

Whiteboard this session. Have the organizational goals front and center and each department's supporting priorities listed under those that you see as being in alignment and having synergy with other functions' goals. This should be a very interactive session, with each person correcting your assumptions, adding, removing, and clarifying the lists. Some of their goals may get moved under a different organizational goal, or they may support more than one.

Whiteboarding each function's goals and initiatives helps you identify shared priorities across teams.

As you work through the exercise, it will become obvious to everyone that some organizational goals are getting support, in varying degrees, from every function. Those are the ones to focus on. You don't want to choose an organizational goal that only one or a few functions are contributing to, leaving other functions out in the cold. If you do that, some functions won't have to change anything while others will have to adopt new goals on top of what they're already doing. Strive for balance so that each function is able to rely on its core competencies and make a greater impact in one area while having less of an impact on another. Everyone should have the opportunity to look like a hero at the end of this, but they should also come away knowing they are going to have to shift focus in some areas to make a real contribution to goals they may not have been focused on previously.

The WIGs may be identical to three organizational goals. However, if any of those bigger goals are not measurable, you will have to define a WIG that is. Each team will then have to figure out how they are going to support that WIG. This doesn't mean they abandon their other priorities. It does mean bringing into focus—and raising the priority of— goals where there is synergy between departments to drive an organizational goal that promotes an optimal customer experience and drives revenue.

This step should also happen in this meeting. Each exec should put forth how, exactly, their function will do its part to satisfy the WIG. Most likely, this will be simply restating a goal or goals that are already on their plate. The important point here is that everyone sees the connection between their goals, other teams' goals, and the WIGs. Achieving those WIGs is everyone's responsibility, and so at this point, they should be on board with supporting one another in any way they can to make those WIGs a reality.

PLANNING

Once the executive team agrees on three WIGs, the planning stage begins. Typically, this is where each executive involved in the WIG development brings together their operational leads to communicate the three goals and start planning how they will support them. These operational leads could be directors, managers, or team leads, depending on the organization.

Just like the executive leadership meeting, this meeting must include all operational leads. How you do this is up to you. You can present them with this initiative and your expectations and ask them to come up with a plan on their own, which they will have to present to you. They may require more guidance from you, in which case you would lead the meeting from start to finish. The goal here is for each operational lead to have a clear plan for supporting one or more of the three WIGs.

Again, the teams will already be making progress toward these WIGs, so you're not going to be turning everyone's life upside down. Rather, you will bring into focus how their work affects revenue. Also, again, they will have the opportunity to realize how their team goals interconnect toward shared goals.

Anytime you introduce change, you're going to be met with pushback. Expect that to happen here, but be heartened by the fact that you are showing people how their work is not just a job or a list of tasks to be completed. They are making a real difference in the company. Their role in these shared goals is integral to customer experience success and, in turn, revenue success.

We talked earlier about how people in today's businesses often feel demoralized, like they cannot make a difference no matter how hard they try. This process may not be the antidote, but it's a step in the right direction.

You and the other executives will address your respective operational leads independently. However, the interconnectivity between the activities of all teams involved in this process should be made clear. No one individual or team is a lone ranger in the process, and their outputs affect someone else's inputs and vice versa. The clearer you can make the relationship between teams to your people, the sooner they will begin to get the holistic overview required to put forth their best efforts as a team.

The value of your RevOps team becomes especially clear here. Since it has visibility and authority over the technology that impacts the customer experience, RevOps will be supporting its internal customers—the Modern Front Office—to facilitate the execution of their plans.

TIMING

How fast you can complete the phases of your Revenue Takeover depends on you, your people, the size of your business, and its culture. This phase, especially, may take a while mainly due to the many people involved. The human element makes predicting a Phase 3 timeline difficult.

With each phase, you have to get more buy-in. If the previous phase was a success, getting people on board with the next phase is a lot easier. At some point, you will have to go to the CEO to tell them their executive team is going to be out for half a day to several days to tackle this whole WIG initiative. If your attempts at Phases 1 and 2 were a struggle, do not expect a hall pass.

The timing also depends on the current level of communication and alignment. A healthy business will be quicker and more agile. One that is disconnected and noncommunicative could take much longer. In general, Phase 3 takes three planning cycles to complete. If you plan annually, expect a three-year timeframe. Since you're focused on annual company goals that could change, you'll have to revisit those and adjust your WIGs and plans accordingly. If you are on a quarterly planning cycle, you'll complete this phase within a year.

Collaborating to come up with an initial plan is a huge accomplishment. If you can do that in the first cycle, celebrate. In the second planning cycle, you'll work through the kinks that you experienced in the first iteration. By that third cycle of planning, this phase has evolved and been adopted as the cultural norm.

Speaking of culture: expect it to change. Getting people to work together on shared goals that result in happier customers who buy more, increasing revenue for the business, leads to happier employees. If they stick with this phase through three cycles, they will not be able to imagine going back to the way they were before the Revenue Takeover.

So far with the Revenue Takeover, you've organized your tech and how it's managed for greater efficiency. That's made your Modern Front Office efforts more productive. Now your people are more connected and more productive, and they are feeling more connected to the business and one another. These steps you are taking will effect positive change that you didn't see coming—side effects of building a better business that's aligned, interconnected, and focused on shared goals. The unprecedented change that's possible with a Revenue Takeover is within your grasp, if you have the courage to make it happen.

OH YES, THERE'S MORE

This third phase, once you complete it, is so revolutionary to your business that you may feel like you couldn't possibly improve upon the Revenue Takeover. At this point, you've torn down a lot of barriers and are working in a more collaborative style with every other CX-related function. The dominos aren't just lined up—they're dancing in the streets.

Still, the heads of Marketing, Sales, Support, Success, and RevOps will continue to have competing priorities and incentives to a degree. Complete alignment and cohesiveness will require one final act: unifying the functions within your Revenue Team under a single point of leadership.

CHAPTER 15

INTRODUCING THE CHIEF REVENUE OFFICER

The most fundamental and important truths at the heart of Extreme Ownership: there are no bad teams, only bad leaders.

—JOCKO WILLINK

Years ago, before getting into the business of marketing, technology, and revenue, Rolly was on staff at USA Volleyball in Colorado Springs, working with the best volleyball teams in the country. Under the governing body for USA volleyball, coaches have ongoing relationships with college coaches, especially those from the top Division I schools. Collaborating and networking on various committees, he met with a lot of coaches.

One coach from a major university caught everyone's attention because he was so well-known. To the outside world, the guy was a winning coach. But being around him, you could see that his management style bordered on abusive. In terms of the science of the sport—motor learning, biomechanics, and exercise physiology—he was doing it all wrong, and his players were paying the price. Uptight, stressed out both physically and mentally, they weren't happy on the team. Many wanted to quit.

The coach wasn't just breaking the rules, he had them all backward. No one could figure out how he kept winning, but we suspected that his players were literally terrified of losing. Trained to take orders instead of thinking for themselves, they were unable to self-manage, and in the long run, weaker players. Eventually, the coach had to step aside. The program crumbled. His team stopped winning, and it was obvious that whatever he had built wasn't sustainable. Though the coach was responsible for building an unhealthy program, he was accountable to someone, and that person was ultimately responsible for ensuring a strong foundation. They failed. Similarly, it's up to you to create that strong foundation that supports healthy growth instead of quick, short-term wins.

There are a lot of ways to "win" in volleyball and in revenue. Some ways crumble when you remove one person or technology. Better approaches don't rely on a single point of success and aren't prone to a single point of failure.

These ways to win increase the effectiveness, quality, and velocity of revenue growth (or volleyball winning) while strengthening the foundation of the organization. They don't crumble when subtracting a person or technology or process. Instead, they create consistency. They stick around—even when times change or times are tough. The new CRO can be a leader of sustainable revenue growth.

SUSTAINABLE, HEALTHY GROWTH

Growth isn't always healthy. At the cellular level, uncontrolled growth is cancer. You can grow your business fast in ways that weaken and destroy it. Have you ever dealt with a Head of Sales or Marketing who got things done by yelling at people, threatening them, punishing them, or scaring them to death? Sure, they get some wins, but their approach isn't healthy or sustainable. Their people and companies pay the price.

You don't want that kind of growth. Your foundation should be healthy and strong, so it lasts no matter who the players are or who's in charge. The right foundation doesn't have single points of failure—it flushes out the weaknesses (like bad coaches and leaders) and survives challenges. It stands up against changes in the market—even global pandemics and economic meltdowns—and rolls with the punches. A strong foundation holds a business up so that even when it's kicked in the pants, it doesn't go down. It catches its breath and keeps going and growing, relying on that foundation and the momentum it's gained to keep building revenue.

Someone has to be accountable for growth. Someone has to have their eye on the prize at all times, building a sustainable platform and ensuring a holistic approach to drive revenue. It cannot be someone who doesn't understand the "physiology" of how revenue is created or someone focused on short-term wins. You need a leader who is committed to building a healthy organization—so strong that it holds itself up so that if they left, it would continue to thrive. The person has to build other people up, train and support them, trust in them, and empower them, so they are all working together to hold the business up.

If you hire the wrong person into that job and they trip and fall, they will take the whole business down with them. You need the right person for that job.

The final phase of the Revenue Takeover, Phase 4, is the creation of the Chief Revenue Officer role. Create the job, identify the responsibilities, assign the team, and adopt the revenue mindset. Then put the right person in charge.

THE REVENUE MINDSET

Historically, Sales has led the revenue charge, and Marketing has supported Sales to that end. With all the changes in the buying landscape, technology, and the customer experience, relying on that model to predict and manage revenue is broken. It just doesn't work. When you shift your view and see the bigger picture, you see that revenue comes from many sources.

However it comes into the business, its main source is outside stakeholders—customers. So rather than focus on the sales team for revenue, let's look at the revenue that comes from customers. The revenue mindset does that: it focuses not on individual players or departments but revenue from customers. How they experience your company has everything to do with how much revenue they're motivated to contribute, and they experience you through various channels, people, and ways.

The revenue mindset removes the boundaries between revenue-generating departments and focuses on how each department works together to optimize revenue. Instead of Marketing looking at Sales when leads don't pan out, the department looks at what Sales needs from them for a better outcome. Instead of Sales looking at Marketing when the leads don't produce deals, they look at how they can help Marketing get the leads they want and what they can do better to follow up on them. There is no blame game because everyone's equally responsible for revenue. At the same time, everyone's empowered and encouraged to communicate, listen, and be willing to change what they're doing to make the revenue goal a reality.

People who adopt the revenue mindset are immediately on a better track for growing revenue. However, as long as they are operating within separate departments and reporting to separate leaders, there will always be opportunities for conflicting stories—what they tell themselves about the status of progress and what they believe needs to happen to ensure revenue goals.

CHIEF REVENUE OFFICER

Beyond alignment, the revenue mindset is about *cohesiveness*. With alignment, you are looking left and right (remember the domino analogy?) to see if what you're doing aligns with everyone else's goals. With cohesiveness, you have visibility into all of your customer interactions. Instead of putting those demands on every member of every team in Marketing, Sales, Support, and Success, a new team is required. This team has the authority to have input on those interactions and manage them holistically for an experience that's consistent. In this way, they can work with other teams to drive an optimal customer experience and create maximum revenue.

This new team needs leadership. A unifying force who understands the customer experience and how it drives revenue is required to lead the charge. Ladies and gentlemen, please allow us to introduce the Chief Revenue Officer.

The Chief Revenue Officer is not the Head of Sales, or the Head of Marketing, or the Chief Financial Officer. They aren't even the CRO the way most people view CROs today, which can vary widely between industries and businesses. In a Revenue Takeover, the CRO is the *Head of ALL Revenue*. They don't sit in an office crunching numbers and analyzing costs, pricing, and margins to figure out how to squeeze maximum dollars out of every sale. This CRO leads the teams and technology that make revenue happen. They don't just track it—they *drive* it.

This is not your grandmother's CRO. It's not even your CRO if you currently have someone with that title. Two situations may give you an idea of what this role encompasses: (1) a startup without the budget—and perhaps, even the need—for a full-blown Head of Sales and Head of Marketing that brings in a person over the sales and marketing directors; and (2) a VP of Sales and Marketing. But even in those cases, the leader may not be directly involved with teams and technology.

WHAT MAKES A GREAT CRO

The CRO role requires a certain kind of person. The ideal candidate has broad interdepartmental knowledge, superior leadership abilities, vision, the fortitude to withstand the demands of immense responsibility, and the resilience to persist through victories and defeats.

KNOWLEDGE

The best CROs have some experience across the five teams that have the greatest impact on customer experience and revenue: Marketing, Sales, Customer Success, Customer Service, and Operations. The CRO may be an expert in only one area, but they require at least some functional knowledge and experience in all of them. They may have picked this up during the evolution of their career, working in and with these departments. They have management experience in more than one department and understand that people in Sales work differently than people in Operations and people in Support.

LEADERSHIP

Don't underestimate the demands of leading people used to working in a particular department. Each has its own culture, work style, daily tasks, and rhythms, and they will bring them to this new team. The CRO has to acknowledge these differences and unite the team under the revenue umbrella in a way that achieves the goal without making everyone want to go back to their old teams.

VISION

Along with a depth of departmental knowledge and leadership skill, a great CRO also must be able to see the big picture and envision how the efforts of their individual team members and other teams that roll up the CRO interconnect to streamline and maximize revenue flow. So while they must have a certain understanding of the details of these processes, they must also know how to remain focused on the holistic net effect and not get lost in those details.

FORTITUDE

The CRO role isn't easy. It's demanding and requires a person with the will, grit, and temperament to withstand the pressures of being accountable for the company's biggest goal. If they've never held a position where you're either "a hero or a zero," they may not have the stomach for it. If they've worked under those circumstances and welcome that responsibility, they may be a good fit.

RESILIENCE

Along with accountability, the CRO has to be able to bounce back no matter what. They cannot be a person who allows failures to hold them back but must instead learn from the letdowns and keep pushing on. The best CRO is agile. They don't get to start from square one and design the perfect team and revenue plan. They have to start with existing resources and plans-in-progress and make them work. They need to be able to think fast on their feet, rebound quickly, and have a strategy and a plan for what's next regardless of any setbacks.

These are huge shoes to fill, and not everyone is cut out to be a CRO, even people with many years of executive experience in tough markets. But for some, Chief Revenue Officer is the role of a lifetime. If you fantasize about what it would be like to combine the best of Marketing, Sales, Customer Success, Customer Service, and Operations—and coalesce their efforts into a well-tuned, revenue-generating machine—you may be a good candidate for CRO.

POTENTIAL CRO CANDIDATES

You may have someone in your ranks who's perfect for the CRO role. Often, the current CMO is in the best position to make the switch. CMOs usually have a lot of experience around the technical requirements. They've worked with numerous channels and interfaced with a lot of teams. The CMO has a good idea how other teams work, and the person may have already worked in or managed Sales, Customer Success, Customer Service, and Operations.

The CMO is used to working under pressure. They may not have as big a target on their back as the Head of Sales, but they understand accountability. The person already has a modern way of looking at revenue strategically, analytically, and technically. The Head of Success may also be a good candidate. This person is used to working across teams, they interface with Marketing, and they're aligned with Sales and Support.

These are just two possible choices, and the best person for your business could come from another function or organizational level. In some instances, the CEO may want to take on the job at least temporarily. If no one fits the bill or wants the job, you can hire a Chief Revenue Officer from outside your business.

Putting the wrong person in the CRO role is worse than putting no one in it. Your first impulse may be to move the Head of Sales into the position, but that is not always a good move. The issue is that Sales, which has always seen itself as the King of Revenue, may not appreciate the benefits of capitalizing on all the new resources at their disposal. The person may not be a good collaborator. And while they may be used to handling the blame of failure, they may not be accustomed to sharing the glory of success. That's not to say that *your* Head of Sales isn't the best fit. If that person loves leading across teams and making five-year plans, and has the depth of knowledge and breadth of vision to bring all the functions and technology of your Revenue Team together in the best way possible, they could be your next CRO.

Whomever you choose to put in the CRO role, and that person could very well be you, they will have to abdicate whatever throne they are currently on—whether it's Sales, Marketing, or something else—to take on the Revenue Throne and all the pain and the glory that accompanies the position.

DIRECT REPORTS OF THE CRO

To be effective, the Chief Revenue Officer requires adequate support and authority to guide strategies that lead to revenue goals. To that end, several department heads should report to this leader, including the VPs of Marketing, Sales, Success, Support, and RevOps. If you have a VP of Customer Experience, think about how that fits. CX is a construct—an outcome of the actions of these other departments. The Chief Revenue Officer will be maximizing revenue through CX created and executed by these departments, so having a separate function isn't necessary. If you have a department like this, they may get rolled into RevOps or another department.

Each functional team still requires management and leadership specific to their skillset, and they will look to their VPs, directors, managers, and team leads for that level of direction. By instating the CRO and putting them in a position over these other groups, you are creating a more holistic entity that gets its marching orders from one person and toward one goal—the generation of revenue. This does not mean that all their other goals and tasks are set by the wayside, but that their jobs will have a new focus and that they will be more transparent and connected in their work toward this shared goal. This approach removes—or at the least minimizes—competing priorities across departments because everyone has the same priority.

People reporting up through this structure aren't all going to be out there selling products unless they're salespeople. They may not be driving revenue directly, but they will be supporting it so others can drive it. By affecting the customer experience, they are supporting the business's ability to make money. It's important to make that point to people when you make this switch because the very word "revenue" will scare them to death. But you can connect the dots for them so they see how their work makes possible the goals of the functional department and the Revenue Team.

Not every leader will be on board with this structure. Executives who have been reporting to a CEO will not like reporting to someone new, especially if it's a colleague with whom they've been engaged in a sort of contentious, internal competition over the years. Some leaders will not like being responsible for revenue. They are just not comfortable having any kind of accountability target on their back, especially one with a conspicuous dollar sign on it. That's way too close for comfort to the CEO's and the company's major goal. Other leaders will want to maintain their silos. Simply put, they do not want to share what they're doing and do not want to be told what to do. They are happy with the status quo, doing exactly what they've always done without having to worry about revenue. Still others will see this move as upsetting their career plans.

However, some will welcome the new model. They will see the opportunity for more productivity within their own department and the chance to contribute to a highly visible company goal. They may even see that they need this help because they cannot operate at their highest level in a vacuum.

You could lose leaders over this. That's a decision they have to make for themselves. Or that decision may have to be made for them in the best interest of the business. If they don't like this new structure, they are probably not the right person to lead your people into the future.

CHANGE IS HARD, BUT IT'S HARDER WHEN YOU DON'T COMMUNICATE

Before we get into how all this rolls out, let's address the alarms going off in your head. We hear them:

This all sounds fantastic, except ARE YOU KIDDING ME? THIS IS HUGE. IT'S MASSIVE. IT'S NOT WHAT WE'VE

BEEN DOING. IT'S DIFFERENT. DO YOU KNOW WHAT HAPPENED WHEN WE SWITCHED COFFEE VENDORS? OR REPLACED CHIPS WITH FRUIT IN THE VENDING MACHINES? PEOPLE HATE CHANGE. THEY. WILL. FREAK. OUT.

Did we get that about right?

First off, you're not going to spring this massive change on people. You can move toward a Revenue Takeover in steps so that by the time you announce the CRO role, the move will seem natural. As you're moving along, talk to your people about how the evolution of the process will roll out so they're not taken by surprise. Then, talk to them about your 100-day plan and show them what the future will look like. Let them know that they will be part of the change, and that by working together they will all be able to do more with fewer roadblocks, less stress, and clearer objectives. They will be helping to provide a superior customer experience that makes the competition look like chumps. And if that isn't enough, they'll be contributing to the company's revenue goals.

THE FIRST 100 DAYS

The CRO will have a lot on their plate with this new role, but three initiatives must take priority for the Revenue Team to succeed: (1) alignment of processes; (2) resetting goals by function; and (3) evaluating resources and structure.

PROCESS ALIGNMENT

Process alignment deals directly with the customer experience. This is where you figure out what has to change in your customer-facing channels to create the ideal customer experience. Back in Chapter 6, "If It Isn't Working for the Customer, It Isn't Working," we talked about what great CX looks like. This is where we make those changes happen. Look at how you're doing with all of this today. Then devise a plan that gets you to a better place. The desired outcome is the best CX you can deliver.

GOAL RESET BY FUNCTION

Once you have a plan for process alignment, reset the goals of each function and team to support those goals. This is described in Chapter 9, "The Domino Effect." Coming out of Phase 3 of the Revenue Takeover, you will already have some alignment, so you won't be starting from scratch here. You will be taking a closer look at how all the dominos line up and the goals in place to give people direction.

EVALUATE RESOURCES AND WORKFORCE STRUCTURE

The third step, once you've completed process alignment and goal setting, is to reevaluate your resources and workforce structure. Based on the changes you've made, does it still make sense? Chapter 10, "The 'Open Concept' Revenue Team," explained the concept of teams without walls. Reporting to the same person doesn't guarantee open communication and collaboration. As long as teams work in silos, the Revenue Takeover won't work.

Teams will change. You will have to create a team to manage the revenue technology and operations, which may not even exist right now. People on other teams may join that team, or they could end up on another team. This isn't about cleaning house—it's about taking a closer look at what your people can do and want to do, and where they would be happiest and best suited to fulfill the goals of the Revenue Team. You might discover that some roles that are currently filled by a single person require a second or even a third person. You might find that some roles can go away completely, but the people in them would be great in other roles. Keep your eye on the revenue goal and figure it out.

TIME TO LEAD

Phase 4 is critical to the success of a Revenue Takeover. Without the right leadership, you won't get the vision, direction, accountability, or support that makes the whole thing work. One person who sees revenue as a direct result of customer experience and can lead the charge, bringing in all the teams that contribute to CX, is the final piece of the puzzle that makes all the other pieces work.

This is a big role. It's an important role, with a lot of visibility and responsibility. Beyond the position and responsibilities, the title is also important. You can't just assign the job to the CMO or the Head of Sales or the Head of Success because people will still see them in their old role. They won't make the connection between the CRO and revenue or the CRO and the customer experience and how they fit in the plan.

That mental shift that began in Phase 1, and gained momentum in Phase 2 and Phase 3, culminates in Phase 4. Naming a Chief Revenue Officer, communicating which departments roll up under this person and are now part of the Revenue Team, and executing on a plan that aligns processes, resets goals, and utilizes people and resources to make it happen completes the process.

If you started reading this thinking it was a revolutionary idea, I hope by now you see that it's more of a natural *evolution*. Someone has to oversee all the revenue—beyond the sales team, beyond online sales, and beyond anyone and anything else that contributes to, oversees, tracks, or measures revenue. It's been a long time coming, and at this point, the need for a Chief Revenue Officer should be crystal clear.

CONCLUSION

Stop acting so small. You are the universe in ecstatic motion.

—RUMI

We didn't start out in the revenue business. We cared about marketing and technology and how we could help businesses integrate the right products into their marketing efforts to create the best customer experience possible. Along the way, our customers grew. We always knew the connection was there; we just didn't realize how much improving the customer experience would impact their businesses. Beyond happier customers and more sales, their businesses *worked* better. Their people worked better, and their cultures improved.

Guiding companies through the different elements of a Revenue Takeover showed us how impactful the process could be. It also showed us that if you don't move ahead, you get behind. Dare to imagine what your company could be. Be brave enough to step into that future. Look to your leaders and your colleagues and see who's on board.

If you're a CEO, give this book to your CMO. Then have a meeting to figure out how you can tackle the Revenue Takeover together. If you're a CMO, have a conversation with your CEO. Show them what's possible. If you need help, reach out. Get the ball rolling, then bring in new staff, consultants, or Revenue Takeover specialists to help finish the job.

Let us know how your Revenue Takeover is going. You will learn more on your adventure than what's in this book because you will be writing your own Revenue Takeover story. Reach out at revenuetakeover.com and tell us your story, your challenges, and your ideas. If you're stuck, let us know. We want you to succeed, and we believe you will.

ACKNOWLEDGMENTS

We would like to acknowledge all the great people who made this book possible.

Thank you to our current Tegrita team members: Ainsley Berry, Amy Noel, Andy Shaw, Ben Parks, Bo Omotayo, Chloe Kelsch, Jason Semenek, Jesse Nobbe, Jessica Jones, Jessica Venerus, Manar Asaya, Max Stoddard, Mythili Viswanathan, Nadim Fetaih, Patrick Galapon, Peter Chen, Rafael de Castro Bueno, Sara Noor, Sarah Sipione, Sheroy Mistry, Sid Sethi, and Tim Happ.

Our families were so supportive during the late nights and long conference calls. They gave us support and space and inspired us to construct our thinking into a cohesive and useful guide for executives around the globe.

Many sincere thanks to our supportive family members: Cadence Starr, Calise Starr, Carmela Geller, Catalina Geller, Charley Keenan, Cienna Starr, Cotrillia Ewing, David Geller, Derrian Brown, Felicia Walker, Jake Keenan, Max Keenan, Nate Keenan, Parker Starr, Rod Starr, Sam Keenan, Solán Wheeler, and Veronica Ramirez.

ABOUT THE AUTHORS

BRANDI STARR, MIKE GELLER, and **ROLLY KEENAN** form the leadership team at Tegrita, a Toronto-based modern marketing technology and strategy consulting firm that serves clients across Canada and the United States.

Brandi is a career strategist, bringing more than two decades of marketing experience to her role as Tegrita's COO. Leveraging technology to drive marketing strategy has always been her major focal point. In 2018, Brandi was named one of MartechExec's "50 Women You Need to Know in Martech." A natural-born overachiever, Brandi was born with two teeth, ready to take a bite out of marketing, technology, and everything else she cares to sink her teeth into. She lives in Atlanta, Georgia, where she claims to survive mostly on tacos, her go-to meal for herself and her family.

Mike Geller, Tegrita's co-founder and CTO, is the firm's principal technologist, with more than fifteen years of marketing tech consultant experience under his belt. Based in Toronto, Mike's a self-proclaimed coffee snob, a Trekkie, a husband, and a proud dad to two children.

Rolly Keenan is Tegrita's CRO and the firm's key growth specialist, with more than twenty years of experience in enterprise software consulting and marketing strategy. A graduate of Northwestern University's Kellogg School of Management, Rolly's also a trained hostage negotiator, a skill he's seldom been called on to use in his current role at Tegrita. He splits his time between Chicago and Colorado with his partner, Veronica, and their blended family of six children and one dog, Nala.

Printed in Great Britain
by Amazon

32978532R00148